REJOICE!
His Promises Are Sure

ARDETH GREENE KAPP

Deseret Book Company, Salt Lake City, Utah

Library of Congress Cataloging-in-Publication Data
  Kapp, Ardeth Greene, 1931–
    Rejoice! His promises are sure / by Ardeth Greene Kapp.
      p.   cm.
    Includes index.
    ISBN 1-57345-233-5 (hardback)
    1. Christian life—Mormon authors. 2. Promises—Religious
  aspects—Christianity. I. Title.
  BX8656.K39   1997
  248.4'89332—dc21   96-50301
                                                                       CIP

Printed in the United States of America

10   9   8   7   6   5   4   3   2   1

*To all those
who yearn to know
that
His promises are sure*

CONTENTS

ACKNOWLEDGMENTS

I would like to thank those who have, over the years, taught me by precept and example that "His promises are sure." The histories recorded by my grandparents, the lives of my parents, the testimonies of my family and friends, the dedication of my teachers, my relationship with my husband, and the witness of the Spirit all give me reason to rejoice in this eternal truth.

I express appreciation to Ronald A. Millett, president of Deseret Book, and Sheri Dew, vice president, for their friendship and support in my writing. A special thanks to Emily Watts, a skilled and compassionate editor, and Kent Ware, a sensitive and astute designer, for their help in preparing this book for publication.

I WILL TRUST IN THEE FOREVER

*S*ome time ago, in a rather remote, heavily wooded area in the far northern part of British Columbia, a dear brother in his late eighties approached me after a meeting in which I had just spoken. His eyes were bright, penetrating, and alive with excitement as he extended his very rough and crusty hand. With a broad smile revealing several missing teeth, he expressed in simple words his unwavering faith and total trust in this grand plan of the gospel of Jesus Christ. He then began describing in detail a project, now almost completed, that had consumed his full attention in recent years. It was a beautiful coffin that he was preparing for his burial.

With enthusiasm, he explained how this project reflected the story of his life. He had constructed a beautiful box from a carefully selected tree. On one side of the box he had painstakingly carved scenes depicting his life as a fisherman. The second side showed him as a lumber man in the logging industry; the third recorded his life as a hunter. With even greater feeling and

emotion, he described in detail the message to be conveyed on the fourth and final side of his coffin. It would show him on his horse going up a steep path to the very top of a mountain. As he spoke, he raised his right arm as high as his stooped frame would allow. His broad, toothless smile continued, but his bright eyes glistened with tears and excitement as he testified in complete trust, "And Mama will be there." He lowered his hand as if in benediction to his testimony.

Then, without even taking a breath to change the subject, he asked, "Oh, and by the way, Sister Kapp, how do you make them words come out of your mouth so smooth-like when you talk? How did you learn to do that?"

I explained to this dear brother: "It sounds smooth-like to you not because of the words but because you have learned to listen with the Spirit, with your heart and your mind. Through your life of fishing and hunting and logging, you have learned to trust in the Lord forever, and that makes everything smooth-like."

Trusting in the Lord—what a difference it makes! "In God We Trust," we read on every coin minted in the United States of America. What did that message mean to those who determined to inscribe it on their country's money? Was it supposed to mean something to all the citizens who would pass those coins from hand to hand in the course of financial affairs? Might it remind us that if we trust in God, we will trust that he, being the Creator of all things, has some idea of what would be best for us? Could it remind us of the guidance he has given on how and where our money should be used and how we should live our lives?

"In God We Trust." Today, unfortunately, much of the world would have us believe that the coin itself is our god, and that we can have anything in this world if we have enough coins—enough prestige, power, possessions, and popularity. Could money be the god we as a people have come to trust in?

At a time when many people seem to be losing trust in the government, in the law, and even in their own friends and family, I am anchored by the powerful words of President Gordon B. Hinckley: "We have nothing to fear. God is at the helm . . . he will shower down blessings upon those who walk in obedience to his commandments." I am convinced that now more than ever before we must be thus reassured. We can have unwavering, unquestionable, undeniable trust in our Father in Heaven.

Nephi, although grieved because of his own iniquities and "encompassed about, because of the temptations and the sins which . . . so easily beset" him, declared, "Nevertheless, I know in whom I have trusted" (2 Nephi 4:18–19). His heart and soul were filled with reassurance. Hear his conviction: "O Lord, I have trusted in thee, and I will trust in thee forever. I will not put my trust in the arm of flesh; for I know that cursed is he that putteth his trust in the arm of flesh. Yea, cursed is he that putteth his trust in man or maketh flesh his arm" (2 Nephi 4:34).

In considering this matter of trust, let us contemplate the trust the Savior must have had in God the Father as we stood at that premortal moment of decision that was to affect all mankind for worlds without end. The Father's plan called for an atoning sacrifice, a Redeemer. To his inquiry, "Whom shall I send?" with unquestioning trust Jesus Christ spoke out and said, "Send me" (see Abraham 3:27). What level of trust in the Father would that have required? And what of the trust the Father had in his Son that he would go all the way—not almost to the cross, not part of the way until he reached Golgotha, but all the way through the infinite and eternal atonement. Think of what that atoning sacrifice means to you and to me individually.

Now, I can understand and expect that level of trust between the Father and the Son, but the concept of trust becomes penetrating to my soul and almost beyond comprehension when I consider the trust the Son must have had in each of us that we would do our part. Having paid that awful price in our behalf, he trusted that it would not be in vain. And even though he knew that some would not repent, would not turn to him and accept the gift of the Atonement, still his trust in the Father's plan was sufficient to carry our Savior and Redeemer all the way through the Garden of Gethsemane to the cross, until at last he could say, "It is finished" (John 19:30).

In the inspiring book *Believing Christ,* author Stephen E. Robinson suggests that not only must we believe that Jesus is who he says he is, we must also believe that he can and will do what he says he can. We must not only *believe in* Christ, we must also *believe* Christ, that we might each be better prepared to say, as did Nephi, "O Lord . . . I will trust in thee forever" (2 Nephi 4:34).

I believe there are three elements that must be in place—three parts to the divine equation, so to speak—for this level of trust to exist. First, we must believe that God can do all things. The scriptures are filled with examples illustrating his grand omnipotence. May I share one such example, in which Heavenly Father's power is demonstrated in two virtually opposite situations, as if to convince us that nothing is impossible with the Lord.

Remember that the Savior, the Son of God, was born of a young virgin. When Mary was approached by the Angel Gabriel announcing the message from God concerning her special mission, her obedient response was: "Behold the handmaid of the Lord; be it unto me according to thy word" (Luke 1:38). What a remarkable and inspiring statement of complete trust!

On the other end of the spectrum, prior to Gabriel's visit to Mary he appeared to Zacharias in the temple to announce that the priest's wife, an old woman stricken in years and barren, would conceive a son in her old age. These two extreme opposite examples—the birth of the Christ child to the young virgin Mary and the promise of a son to aged and barren Elisabeth— suggest something of the scope, the depth, the breadth of the Father's plan, and the reach that is extended to accomplish it. To Mary's question, "How shall this be?" the angel responded, "For with God nothing shall be impossible" (Luke 1:34, 37). He can do all things.

Second, we must understand that God has a plan for our happiness that involves covenants and promises. Is there anyone who has not memorized and repeated over and over the message in Proverbs, "Trust in the Lord with all thine heart; and lean not unto thine own understanding. In all thy ways acknowledge him, and he shall direct thy paths" (Proverbs 3:5–6).

The path will not always be easy, but when we face difficult times we must turn toward our Father in Heaven, not away from him. The words of the hymn express it so well:

> *In the furnace God may prove thee,*
> *Thence to bring thee forth more bright,*
> *But can never cease to love thee;*
> *Thou art precious in his sight.*
> *God is with thee,*

God is with thee;
Thou shalt triumph in his might.

(*Hymns,* no. 43)

Elder Neal A. Maxwell reminds us: "Giving up on God and on oneself constitutes simultaneous surrender to the natural man. Daily hope is vital, since the 'Winter Quarters' of our lives are not immediately adjacent to our promised land either. An arduous trek still awaits, but hope spurs weary disciples on. . . . Jesus waits 'with open arms to receive' those who finally overcome by faith and hope (Morm. 6:17). His welcome will consist not of a brief, loving pat, but, instead, of being 'clasped in the arms of Jesus'! (Morm. 5:11)" (*Ensign,* November 1994, p. 36).

Third, when we can be trusted to do our part, such a small portion of this great equation, then we must know that our Father will do his. Not only *can* God bless us, but when we do our part he *will* bless us. He is bound by his own law to do so. We are a covenant people. He tells us, "I, the Lord, am bound when ye do what I say; but when ye do not what I say, ye have no promise" (D&C 82:10).

King Benjamin reminds us of the covenant we have made and the blessings promised us as a result: "Therefore, I would that ye should be steadfast and immovable, always abounding in good works [our part], that Christ, the Lord God Omnipotent, may seal you his, that you may be brought to heaven, that ye may have everlasting salvation and eternal life [his promise to us]" (Mosiah 5:15). Through our baptismal covenant, we have taken upon us his name, with a promise to always remember him and keep his commandments so we can always have his Spirit to be with us. He says to us, as a kind, loving Father, "My son, my daughter, there are some laws, some absolutes. You must do your part. Bring your broken heart and your contrite spirit and I will make you whole. My grace is sufficient to make up the difference."

Any time we seem to be wavering in our trust in the Lord—not for what he *can* do, but for what he *will* do—closer examination may reveal that our lack of trust is not directed toward our Father in Heaven or his Son Jesus Christ as much as toward ourselves. Yet in our individual responsibility and agency to do our part, we are not left alone. We are constantly coached and encouraged to ask for what we need and to remember what we have received. Have you noticed how many times in the scriptures we are counseled to remember, remember? Alma, speaking to his son Helaman, repeats over and over, "O remember, remember, my son" (see Alma 37:13, 14, 32, 35). Later, Helaman repeats the counsel to his own sons, Nephi and Lehi, "Now, my sons, remember, remember" (Helaman 5:12).

Our trust is increased through our studying the scriptures and remembering the instruction from our Savior, he who marked the path and led the way. We remember him when we feast, study, and ponder upon his words daily. We remember him when we pray, not just saying the words but pouring out our hearts with our specific longings, so that when our prayers are answered we can recognize the Lord's hand in those answers. We remember him when we partake of the sacramental bread and water, those sacred emblems that remind us of our covenants. We remember him in the springtime, in the miracles of rebirth, new life, new promise of the resurrection. We remember him in the summer, for he is the light and the life. We remember him in the fall, when the blossoms are gone and the roots of the trees reach deep into the soil in preparation for another season. We remember him in the winter, when we walk by faith, knowing that there will be yet another spring.

Yes, we are counseled to remember, and we are also invited, over and over, to ask. Is it possible that any of us might be carrying an unnecessarily heavy burden because we failed to ask for help? Asking is essential to our part of the equation if we are to trust in the Lord.

If our level of trust were dependent on our own resources and ability, we would be forever lost and discouraged as we struggled with the natural man, our imperfections, our failings, our inadequacies. Fortunately, our trust is not in the arm of flesh but in the Lord. This may be a hard lesson to learn. We may find ourselves asking, "Where do I begin?" The answer is yet another evidence of God's love for us and his desire to bless us. He will take us wherever we are at this moment: "Even if ye can no more than desire to believe, let this desire work in you, even until ye believe in a manner that ye can give place for a portion of my words" (Alma 32:27).

Here, then, is the whole equation, the formula for our trusting in the Lord. We know what God can do. We know that he has a plan for our happiness and salvation. And we know what we must do and what he will do to help us do our part.

The key factor that makes the equation viable is the atonement of Jesus Christ. The whole plan hinges on that sacrifice. So the final question we might ask ourselves as we strive to develop trust in the Lord is "Why?" Why did he put himself in a position of helpless mortality, to "suffer temptations, and pain of body, hunger, thirst, and fatigue, even more than man can suffer, except it be unto death" (Mosiah 3:7)? Why did he endure the agony of Gethsemane and sweat drops of blood from every pore? In the hour of his final suffering, his focus was never for a moment on himself. In those last moments of his life, amid those who spat on him, mocked him, scourged him, and plaited a crown of thorns for his head, he said, "Father, forgive them; for they know not what they do" (Luke 23:34). It has been said that it was not nails that held Jesus on the cross but his love for us. Because of his love for us—sinner and saint and everyone in between—he went all the way and made it possible for each of us to go all the way.

Can there be any question about his willingness to see us through, however long the road or however far we may be from the path? I think of the little Bolivian woman who, upon hearing the grand gospel plan explained by the missionaries, looked up from under her tiny hat and questioned, "You mean, he did that for me?" The Spirit testified to her of this great eternal truth, and then not in question but in testimony she whispered with emotion and conviction, "He did that for me." "He was wounded for our transgressions, he was bruised for our iniquities; the chastisement of our peace was upon him; and with his stripes we are healed" (Isaiah 53:5).

The Apostle Paul reminds us, and may we never forget, "Ye are bought with a price" (1 Corinthians 6:20). There is no question: Not only can he bless us, love us, forgive us, and heal us, but he wants to. When we can be trusted to do our small part in this enormous equation, he will do all the rest, everything needed, nothing lacking. Of his character we read: "His forgiveness was unbounded, his generosity was untiring, his patience was inexhaustible, his mercy was immeasurable, his courage was illimitable, his wisdom was unfathomable, his kindness was

interminable, his faith removed mountains, his hope had no shadow in it, his love was infinite. He is the ideal of the heart. He is the goal of humanity" (Charles Edward Jefferson, *The Character of Jesus* [New York: Parliament Publishing, 1968], p. 352).

On those occasions when we feel least worthy, when the Lord shows unto us our weaknesses and we may become discouraged, let us remember the words of Nephi: "Yea, why should I give way to temptations, that the evil one have place in my heart to destroy my peace and afflict my soul? Why am I angry because of mine enemy? Awake, my soul! No longer droop in sin. . . . Rejoice, O my heart, and cry unto the Lord, and say: O Lord, I will praise thee forever; yea, my soul will rejoice in thee, my God, and the rock of my salvation" (2 Nephi 4:27–30). That trust began in the grand council when we cast our vote: "O Lord, I will trust in thee forever. I did then. I do now. And I will forever." Let our voices echo down through the generations of time as we join with Nephi and all the faithful Saints in expressing our trust in God.

THE THREE BUSHES

In the book of Exodus, we read that Moses came to the mountain of God, and "the angel of the Lord appeared unto him in a flame of fire out of the midst of a bush: and he looked, and, behold, the bush burned with fire, and the bush was not consumed. . . . God called unto him out of the midst of the bush, and said, Moses, Moses. And he said, Here am I. And he said, Draw not nigh hither: put off thy shoes from off thy feet, for the place whereon thou standest is holy ground" (Exodus 3:2–5). The Pearl of Great Price adds these words of the Lord to Moses: "Behold, thou art my son; . . . and I have a work for thee" (Moses 1:4, 6). And then he gave this all-encompassing declaration: "This is my work and my glory—to bring to pass the immortality and eternal life of man" (Moses 1:39).

Will we ever find a high mountain, a burning bush, and hear a voice in our minds and in our hearts? Will God speak to us? Indeed he will—he wants to. He is beckoning to each of us: "Draw near unto me and I will draw near unto you; seek me diligently and ye shall find me; ask, and ye shall receive; knock, and it shall be opened unto you" (D&C 88:63). Could there be a message more inviting, more welcoming? He continues with an admonition accompanied by a remarkable and soul-stirring promise: "Therefore, sanctify yourselves that your minds become single to God, and the days will come that you shall see him; for he will unveil his face unto you, and it shall be in his own time, and in his own way, and according to his own will" (D&C 88:68). This speaks to my heart as though it were a welcome-home message. God is our Father. We are his children, and one day we shall see him and be with him.

The message of the burning bush is relevant to us today in our personal lives. God will speak to us. When we think of the mountain of the Lord, surely we are reminded of the temple, where we can go with any question or concern or burden and he will speak peace to our minds. Other private places may also be appropriate for our ponderings. We may not find immediate answers, but we'll feel peace while we wait upon the Lord. This is the promise of the burning bush.

And now, let us consider the message of the currant bush. Perhaps you remember the graphic illustration given by President Hugh B. Brown of his personal experience with a currant bush. President Brown told of having purchased a farm in Canada. One morning he saw a currant bush on his farm that had grown to be about six feet high and needed pruning, so he cut it back to "nothing but a little clump of stumps." Then, in his words:

> I thought I saw on top of each of these little stumps . . . a tear, and I thought the currant bush was crying. . . . I looked

at it, and smiled, and said, "What are you crying about?" You know, I thought I heard that currant bush talk. And I thought I heard it say this: "How could you do this to me? I was making such wonderful growth. . . . I thought you were the gardener here." . . . I said, "Look, little currant bush, I *am* the gardener here, and I know what I want you to be. I didn't intend you to be a fruit tree or a shade tree. I want you to be a currant bush, and some day, little currant bush, when you are laden with fruit, you are going to say, 'Thank you, Mr. Gardener, for loving me enough to cut me down, for caring enough about me to hurt me. Thank you, Mr. Gardener.'"

President Brown went on to tell of a very difficult and discouraging time in his life, a disappointing time when he felt cut down and found himself saying, "How could you do this to me, God? I have done everything I could to measure up." Then, he said: "I heard a voice, and I recognized the tone of this voice. It was my own voice, and the voice said, 'I am the gardener here. I know what I want you to do.'" The bitterness went out of his soul, and he fell to his knees. "God is the gardener here," President Brown concludes his story. "He knows what he wants you to be" (*New Era*, January 1973, pp. 14–15).

I trust each of us knows something of the results of pruning: not scars to destroy us, but spiritual refinement to enable us to become what God intends us to become. Jesus Christ is the Gardener, and he promises not only immortality but eternal life to any who will become "as a child, submissive, meek, humble, patient, full of love, willing to submit to all things which the Lord seeth fit to inflict upon him, even as a child doth submit to his father" (Mosiah 3:19). Note that the scripture specifies submitting to *all* things. The Gardener who loves us will cut us back, cut us down, put us in hard places—he will strip us of our pride, whatever the cost.

Now I should like to draw close to you and sit side by side near the beautiful forsythia bush that opened my mind and my heart some time ago in Canada. When my husband was called to preside over the Canada Vancouver Mission, we were aware that during our three years of service we would have approximately 450 young men and women entrusted to our care. He had never been a mission president before, and I'd never been a mission president's wife. We had not even the benefit of being parents. We were eager to live by the Spirit, teach by the Spirit, testify by the Spirit, and better understand the workings of the Spirit so that we could accomplish the work of the Lord. We examined ourselves and felt the need for a cleansing so that nothing would lessen our communication, our direction, and our ability to listen to the whisperings of the Spirit related to this sacred calling. The lines from a hymn by Eliza R. Snow seemed to set the stage for our launching:

> *Be fixed in your purpose, for Satan will try you;*
> *The weight of your calling he perfectly knows.*
> *Your path may be thorny, but Jesus is nigh you;*
> *His arm is sufficient, tho demons oppose.*
> *His arm is sufficient, tho demons oppose.*
>
> (Hymns, no. 266)

I soon discovered that the setting for the first round of the battle with the enemy is that you see all of your weaknesses illuminated and magnified, including some you didn't even know you had, and others you thought you had mastered years ago.

After the initial discouragement, you take comfort in realizing that the Lord, knowing all those things about you, called you anyway and will stand by you. I was reassured as I read expressions of similar feelings from others; for instance, I took comfort in these words of Elder James E. Faust:

> During the years of my life, and often in my present calling, and especially during a recent Gethsemane, I have gone to my knees with a humble spirit to the only place I could for help. I often went in agony of spirit, earnestly pleading with God to sustain me in the work I have come to appreciate more than life itself. I have, on occasion, felt the terrible aloneness of the wounds of the heart, of the sweet agony, the buffetings of Satan, and the encircling warm comfort of the Spirit of the Master.
>
> I have also felt the crushing burden, the self-doubts of inadequacy and unworthiness, the fleeting feeling of being forsaken, then of being reinforced an hundredfold. I have climbed a spiritual Mount Sinai dozens of times seeking to communicate and to receive instructions. It has been as though I have struggled up an almost real Mount of Transfiguration and upon occasion felt great strength and power in the presence of the Divine. A special sacred feeling has been a sustaining influence and often a close companion. (*Ensign*, November 1976, p. 59)

One kind of spiritual growth and refinement comes when we deal with disappointments and unfulfilled expectations and problems for which we are not responsible. Yes, we must accept and cope and adjust, but there's nothing we can do to change the situation; it's "not our fault," so to speak.

It is quite another kind of spiritual growing to deal with

feelings and circumstances we *are* responsible for, such as pride, feelings of inadequacy, hypocrisy, not being all that others think we are, selfishness, loneliness, misunderstandings, and many other private battles of our own making as we strive to overcome the weaknesses of the flesh.

Early one spring morning, during one of my own times of being pruned and cut back, of struggling and going through a growing season, I knelt in the living room in the mission home by the couch in front of the east windows. On the wall to the left hung a picture of the Savior in the Garden of Gethsemane and one of the Prophet Joseph Smith. I had knelt there many times, pondering the atonement of Christ and the mission of the Prophet Joseph. On this particular day I felt like Enos: My soul hungered, and I cried in mighty prayer and supplication, wanting to hear the voice of the Lord in my mind and in my heart.

After my prayer, I followed my usual path on my morning walk, heading east for several blocks, then north. My heart was heavy with goals not reached, efforts that seemingly bore little fruit, misunderstandings, some young lives wandering off the path, and a sense of responsibility that seemed overwhelming. I walked along the street beside a wooden fence, and at the corner where the fence ended I observed for the first time a very large bush, a forsythia bush, bursting into bloom. I leaned on the fence next to the bush to pause, ponder, evaluate, meditate, and pray. Then I waited.

In time it was as though the bush spoke to me, but not of pruning, like the currant bush. The message of the forsythia bush seemed to be: "After the cold season of winter, if you endure it well, there will be an early spring." And at that moment the bush seemed to burst into a brightness unlike anything I had

ever seen before—a brilliance that brought to my mind thoughts of the burning bush. Was this really occurring, I questioned, or was I imagining it? I turned from the bush and looked down the street. The rays from the early morning sun were centered parallel to the road and rested exactly in line with the bright yellow forsythia bush. A warmth penetrated from the soles of my feet to the top of my head. I shall never forget the brilliance of the sun that morning and the illumination that seemed to radiate from within the bush. I lingered for some time, until the morning rays passed over.

I returned home that spring morning with renewed faith and hope, with a desire for greater charity. My soul was touched, and I would ever after sing with greater meaning the words to the hymn:

> *Thy Spirit, Lord, has stirred our souls,*
> *And by its inward shining glow*
> *We see anew our sacred goals*
> *And feel thy nearness here below.*
> *No burning bush near Sinai*
> *Could show thy presence, Lord, more nigh.*
>
> (*Hymns*, no. 157)

Summer came, and fall, and Christmas. Things were now running smoothly in the mission. But our battle with the adversary is never over. He changes his tactics, trying anything to disarm his enemies. In January, Heber became seriously ill and had to be rushed to the hospital. Now, I'm not suggesting that his illness was the work of the adversary, but it is easy to be less fixed in your purpose if you can be distracted, even justifiably so, with other concerns. And to distract our attention from our course, our purpose, is a tactic of the enemy.

In our case, rather than worry about having to return home before we had finished the work we had been sent to do, we chose to become recommitted to our purpose and to guard against any tiny seeds of doubt that could grow up and pollute the soil where a forsythia bush might otherwise take root. Heber's speedy recovery was something of a miracle, with no ill effects.

January and February passed quickly and we came back around to March, the springtime of the year. Once again I found myself in the living room on my knees, expressing gratitude for so many blessings and for the growth that comes during the wintertimes of our lives. On this day I walked my usual path around the block until I came to the wooden fence. I stopped at the corner by the forsythia bush, which was once again in bloom. The morning sun was bright and the blossoms abundant. But the forsythia bush was quiet. There was no message this time, no illumination, just a pretty bush. It had been a season of growth for me, and the light at this time came not from the forsythia bush, as bright as it was, but rather from the writings of Isaiah: "The sun shall be no more thy light by day; neither for brightness shall the moon give light unto thee: but the Lord shall be unto thee an everlasting light, and thy God, thy glory" (Isaiah 60:19).

Our three years were too quickly coming to a close. Our mission was known as the "mountaintop mission," and we had observed and participated in some pretty steep climbs. We had learned that when you find your Sinai and climb it, climb it to

the top, God will speak to you in your heart and mind, with or without a burning bush.

Listen to the words of a young elder who wrote his feelings at the close of his mission: "I have discovered that as I am obedient there is an inner strength and peace that comes. This feeling can prevail despite the turmoil and strife that may be going on. I have learned how the Lord answers our prayers and prepares us for coming events." That young elder who knew about the burning bush had experienced the currant bush and was blessed with the light from the forsythia bush.

In our daily experiences, we will have those moments when we hear the Lord speak to us from the burning bush. We must endure our currant-bush experiences, humbly submitting to the pruning knife. We will experience the radiance of the forsythia bush and be reminded that the light from within comes through the workings of the Spirit. "And if your eye be single to my glory, your whole bodies shall be filled with light, and there shall be no darkness in you; and that body which is filled with light comprehendeth all things" (D&C 88:67).

THE INVITATION

sk any missionary, and he or she will tell you that mail is like manna from heaven, usually enough to sustain you but never more than you need. One day in the mission field I received a bit of that manna, an official letter from Church headquarters. I recognized the logo; in fact, I had used that same stationery myself not too many years before. But this time it was different: I was receiving the letter instead of sending it. I quickly tore open the envelope without benefit of a letter opener, as I had seen the missionaries do so often.

At first glance I recognized it as a form letter, but a quick look told me that it bore the actual signatures of dear friends and great leaders. Although I had seen many such letters in the past, and even signed some on occasion, this official invitation awakened an unexpected sense of excitement within me. In fact, as I read the contents, my mind began to conjure up all sorts of possibilities. This one-page letter signed by the general Relief Society presidency was an invitation for me and my special guests to attend the general women's meeting to be held in the Tabernacle in Salt Lake City.

As I looked at the signatures of these friends whom I had been accustomed to calling by their first names during our years of working together, I thought of Elaine and Chieko and Aileen and their thoughtfulness in inviting me to the women's meeting even though they knew I would not be able at this time to accept the invitation. Just the idea of being invited really made me feel good.

As I pondered this gathering to take place in Salt Lake City on Temple Square, remembering all the excitement associated with such an event, my mind took flight and I thought of the many women whom I would like to include as my special guests if I were to attend the conference. I thought of the sisters I had learned to love and admire in this new location, some of them in the far northern part of the province of British Columbia. Many would never have the opportunity to go to Salt Lake, to be in the historic Tabernacle, or to meet these leaders, these friends of mine.

One of my new friends, Karen Kochel, wears a scar on the side of her face from a large chain saw that got away while she was assisting her father in logging. I thought of being in her home and experiencing there the beauties of cultural things: fine music, beautiful art pieces, her own handicraft of exquisite delicacy. She had also learned the skill of slaughtering pigs to supplement the family income and assist neighbors in need. At one time when she was seven months pregnant, she could be found riding her horse to round up the cattle in a beautiful forested area where her husband carried on a large logging operation. I would certainly invite her to accompany me to the conference.

I saw in my mind another friend. She and her husband lived with their children on a boat. They provided fresh fish, enough for everyone, when the Saints gathered from great distances for Church meetings or socials.

In my mind I walked into the remarkable home of another friend, a beautiful log cabin with every log personally selected and cut, the grain of the wood magnified by hand polishing and skilled craftsmanship. I envisioned this new friend standing at her door, opening her heart and her home to me.

I thought of the welcome we received when we first accepted the invitation to visit Vanderhoof, a location even farther north in Canada than Horsefly or 150 Mile House. It wasn't a city—it was hardly even a town—but it was a wonderful place. We were met on the brow of a hill overlooking an expanse of beauty where the sky meets the earth and splendor reaches out in all directions. A couple in their horse-drawn carriage welcomed us. She was wearing a red silk dress with a long, full skirt and a lovely hat. He was dressed in black tails and a high silk hat. The horse was well groomed and the harness polished. The driver held the long reins in gloved hands.

Heber and I took our seats behind the driver in a padded seat just right for two. After we were settled, Sister Albertson placed a beautiful, handmade, white lap robe over our knees to take care of any chill that might be in the air. As we listened to the clip-clop of the horses' hooves going down the country road, I was humbled by the special effort that had been expended to make this a memorable visit for us. What if we hadn't accepted the invitation? What if at the last minute we had decided not to go because it was not convenient or something else seemed more important?

Invitations often come at a great price. Three hundred or more sisters would be gathering in Victoria on beautiful Vancouver Island on the day of the general women's meeting in Salt Lake City. They were going to make a day of it, beginning at noon and continuing throughout the afternoon with activities, messages, and music that would center on the theme "Because I Have Been Given Much, I Too Must Give." Then, in the evening, by satellite broadcast, they would be able to witness the events of the conference in Salt Lake City.

I thought again of the letter, the special invitation I had received to attend the conference. Immediately a wonderful idea formed in my head and fantasy played on my thoughts. Yes, I would accept the invitation for me and my special guests. There was no question in my mind that when we arrived in Salt Lake there would be room in everyone's hearts and homes for us. About three hundred would be the number of reserved seats I would request in the great Salt Lake Tabernacle on Temple Square. Although I knew from firsthand experience what kind of problems such a gathering would create, still the fantasy of it all, the thought of arriving at the gates of Temple Square with my dear friends, would not leave my mind. Oh, wouldn't it be fun? I thought. How much would it cost? What price would we pay? Would everyone I invited accept the invitation if I could provide the way?

Other thoughts played in my mind: How much is an invitation worth? What if you were never invited? What if you were invited and didn't accept the invitation when such a price had been paid for your benefit and blessing?

The day of the satellite broadcast arrived. Sisters had come from some distance in anticipation of all the preconference

activities. The displays, the music, the gifts and talents so artistically presented and generously shared all helped prepare us for the event. Later, the wonderful blessing of modern technology would allow us to see the proceedings and, more importantly, to feel the spirit of the general women's meeting.

I had been scheduled to address the gathering in Victoria in the early afternoon. In my opening remarks, I told these wonderful sisters about the official invitation I had received for me and my special guests. I informed them, with a smile, that I had sent a fax requesting a reserved seat for each one of them. The audible response was wonderful. There was no question in my mind that, had it been for real, somehow, some way they would all have accepted such an invitation. In my imagination I could envision all of us there on time, in place, filling every seat reserved for us with no one missing.

At 5:00 P.M. the satellite broadcast began. The first view was of the great Tabernacle organ; then the swelling sounds of the music seemed to remove the distance and carry us right there. One of the sisters near the front of our group in Victoria asked with excitement loud enough for everyone to hear, "Where are our reserved seats?" A warm ripple swept over the audience as Sister Elaine Jack explained how sisters were linked together by satellite in the United States, Canada, and many other parts of the world. It was as though the distance had diminished and we were all together for a brief moment in one place. We had responded to the invitation. There was room in the Tabernacle for all of us, for everyone from everywhere. The spirit of sisterhood filled every space.

I thought of other women who might have been invited, ones I'd have liked to sit beside. Eliza R. Snow, Emma Smith,

Lucy Mack Smith, Mary Fielding Smith, my own mother and grandmother, and many others who had paved the way years before would surely have reserved seats. I pondered quietly and reverently. The sense of their presence seemed real to me. It may be presumptuous, but I like to think that those sisters would make room on their bench for me and for you, for all of us.

I understood as never before why an invitation is sent out, even if you can't come. You can carry it in your pocket and know that if you arrived at the door you would be welcomed in and there would be a place for you.

President Howard W. Hunter said, "I would hope that every adult member would be worthy of—and carry—a current temple recommend, even if proximity to a temple does not allow immediate or frequent use of it" (*Ensign*, July 1994, p. 5). In this case, carrying the invitation is a statement of acceptance, whether you can make it to an actual temple or not.

If you received a formal invitation to the Lord's banquet and were invited to feast at his table, would you accept? Would you have time in your schedule? Would there be other events or happenings that would draw you away? Would your reserved seat be empty because of other pressing matters?

Would we all RSVP and be there? Would we bring any guests with us? Or might we be hesitant to ask, for fear that they may not accept or understand? Do you know people who might accept such an invitation if it came personally from you? Whom will you invite this week to feast at a banquet, a holy celebration, a sacrament service, or an individual get-together to read and ponder and pray about the scriptures?

This matter of extending invitations to everyone so that no one is left out is crucial to our blessings. These marvelous

blessings, these invitations, are of the Spirit. When we open our mouths, the Spirit puts the words there, and those who are prepared will respond. As members of The Church of Jesus Christ of Latter-day Saints, we are authorized agents of the Lord, privileged to extend invitations to the living and the dead. The Spirit transcends time and space.

The Lord reminds us: "Remember the worth of souls is great in the sight of God. . . . And if it so be that you should labor all your days in crying repentance unto this people, and bring, save it be one soul unto me, how great shall be your joy with him in the kingdom of my Father! And now, if your joy will be great with one soul that you have brought unto me into the kingdom of my Father, how great will be your joy if you should bring many souls unto me!" (D&C 18:10, 15–16).

We have each received an invitation for us and our special guests. There will be reserved seats and room for everyone when we do our part. Let us accept his invitation and extend it to all around us, that there may be no empty chairs at the banquet of the Lord.

OVERLOOKING
THE TATTOOS

ne January day I learned that there are Winter Quarters experiences in our lives even when we are in the line of duty—maybe even more so at such times, since the adversary works hard to thwart our purpose. Would you walk with me briefly down a thorny path from which I learned a penetrating lesson of faith, hope, and especially charity.

It was Saturday morning, and my husband, Heber, and I were eating breakfast with the foreign-language-speaking missionaries in the Canada Vancouver Mission. Heber was serving as mission president, and had been enjoying excellent health with remarkable endurance as he attended to the multitude of responsibilities relating to the work of the mission. But just as we finished our breakfast that day, he experienced a sudden and severe pain in his back. By Sunday morning, he was in excruciating pain and could not move from the bed. With great concern, I called for an ambulance; paramedics soon arrived and took him to the emergency room of a nearby hospital. Of course I was anxious, but not until I heard the doctor's sobering prognosis did I become alarmed. My world seemed to stop for a moment as I tried to listen to the doctor and understand some frightening possibilities. My worries consumed my every thought, affecting even my breathing. I tried to take deep breaths to ease my anxiety.

Around noon, Heber was moved from the emergency room into room 366, where three of the four beds were already occupied. As the nurses wheeled him into place, I followed closely behind, evaluating the surroundings and the situation. In the bed closest to us was an old man whose scanty clothing revealed dark tattoos the full length of both arms. He looked emaciated, and one of his eyes was distorted and drawn to one side. Quick to judge, I decided right away that I didn't want to be there. *There must be a better place for us*, I thought, *more private, more appropriate, more desirable, where I could feel more peace.*

There in the hospital, a long way from home and feeling alone and anxious, I closed my eyes in prayer. I poured out my heart, speaking of my concern, my anxiety, my fear, my sense of helplessness. Feeling somewhat frantic, I yearned for instant assurance that things would turn out all right. As I continued my earnest supplication, into my mind came the words, "You reach out to those around you, and I will take care of you."

I opened my eyes. The closest one of "those around me" was the old derelict whom I had judged and rejected. Could that man in the bed across the aisle be the one I should reach out to? How could I be concerned for him when I was so consumed with Heber's health and our welfare? Again the thought came, "You reach out to those around you, and I will take care of you."

After a while, I forced myself to speak to the old man. He sat up on the edge of his bed. His speech was slurred as he responded to my questions. I learned that he'd been in the hospital for four months, that he had no friends, no family, and no visitors. He seemed hesitant yet anxious to talk—cautious, but willing. He asked me what I was reading. When I told him it was a book about the saving doctrine of the Book of Mormon, he was quick to respond and asked if he could borrow it when I was finished. He had once been a Mormon, he told me. I walked across the narrow aisle between the beds—a space that at first I had wished were much wider—and handed him the book. This man, who was clearly suffering spiritually as well as physically, reached out for it with both hands like a hungry man reaching for a slice of bread. Maybe he remembered that it contained the bread of life.

He now was eager to ask questions. "Who is the President of the Church now?" he wanted to know. I told him it was President Howard W. Hunter, to which he responded by way of inquiry and interest and with a tone of reverence in his voice, "Oh, did the other guy die?" He struggled to find a photograph that he wanted me to see, a picture of himself in Tonga as a young and handsome man. I wondered at what point along the way he had lost hope, and who might have been there to share the kind of message that can penetrate even the darkest clouds when understood. I heard in my mind the words of Peter, "Be ready always to give an answer to every man that asketh you a reason of the hope that is in you with meekness and fear" (1 Peter 3:15). Was it too late to share a message of hope with him?

Around 9:00 P.M., I excused myself to get Heber a drink; I

needed to find him a straw because he could not sit up. As I was scouting around for one, the thought came to my mind: *Maybe the old gentleman would like a drink.* I got a glass of cool water for him from the fountain. He mumbled what I think must have been an expression of thanks.

When the night nurse came in an hour or so later, the old man gestured toward Heber's bed and instructed her in his halting manner to bring in a big lounge chair. The nurse quickly put him off, explaining that that would not be necessary because Mr. Kapp was far too sick to be sitting up. The man insisted, finally managing to convey to the nurse that the chair was not for Mr. Kapp but for me. He told her where he had seen a big chair that she could move in, and she responded to his request. When she returned, he cranked his bed up into a sitting position, which seemed an effort for him, and instructed her on where it should be located and how to tip it back for my comfort. The nurse left, turning out all the lights except for a dim night light. I thanked my new friend for his concern for me.

Lying back in the big chair, now more comfortable than otherwise would have been possible, I continued my earnest prayer for Heber and found myself also praying for the old man in the bed across the way. The man with the tattoos. Somehow during those long, anxious hours his tattoos had faded from my mind. I saw with different eyes, with a more understanding heart. His eyes were sad but not distorted. His speech was slow but not slurred. He did not appear to me to be the one whom I had so quickly judged and rejected. The lights were low; the book I had loaned him was lying by his bed. I dozed off.

During the night the nurses quietly and frequently came and went. I observed that around 3:00 A.M. the curtain was drawn around the old man's bed. In the early morning, sensing some urgency in the movement of the nurses, I stepped out of the room briefly. When I returned, they were wheeling out a large cart with a heavy cover, heavier than a sheet. The curtain was open and the bed where the old man had slept was empty. He was not there.

There was a cleaning lady standing in the corner who I knew spoke very little English. I asked her where the patient had gone. With tears in her eyes, she raised the palms of her hands and shook her head. "Gone," she whispered, "gone." The nurses confirmed her message: The old man had died during the night.

I pondered the events of that last evening. His last act, his last word had been one of concern for someone else's welfare. *My* welfare. My eyes filled with tears; my heart was full. I wished I had spoken to him sooner, taken him drinks more often. I wished I had offered to read to him from the book instead of just loaning it to him. Now he was gone, and the opportunity had passed. I realized that the tattoos that had caused my initial rejection of the old man were not on the surface of his skin but within my heart, judgments that had clouded my vision.

Heaven seemed very close in that hospital room. I had a deep feeling for the old man. *Maybe, just maybe,* I thought, *I was privileged to perform the last act of service for him in a simple glass of cool water.* I thought of living water that quenches spiritual thirst, that comforts and heals and gives hope in troubled times. I thought of the book I had loaned him about the bread of life and living water. The book was not on the small table where he had placed it the night before. The nurses said it had been taken with one or two other things, his only earthly possessions. I explained that I had loaned him the book, and it was later returned to me.

When I look at that book now, the words return to my mind with increasing clarity: "You reach out to those around you, and I will take care of you."

And, as always, the Lord's promise was sure. Heber was blessed with a miraculous healing. The doctor had originally explained that the best he could hope for was a slow recovery involving three to six weeks of hospital care. The following Sunday, one week later, through the power of a priesthood blessing, Heber was released from the hospital. The doctor, unable to provide an explanation, spoke of a miracle and marveled at the speed of his recovery. And I too had experienced a kind of healing. The old man whom I had so quickly judged and rejected was out of reach, but my heart had been softened and changed.

About two months later, Heber and I attended a district conference in the northern part of Vancouver Island. I spoke briefly of the things we had experienced during Heber's illness, particularly the important lesson I had learned from the man with the tattoos. The woman who was asked to give the closing prayer in that meeting was, as the stake president explained, a less-active member whom he had felt inspired to call on. This dear sister made her way to the front. I saw her trembling hands as she placed them on either side of the pulpit. Haltingly she expressed gratitude and appreciation, and then closed with these words: "And help us, O Lord, that we might love one another and overlook the tattoos."

I shall never forget the lesson of faith, hope, and charity that I learned in room 366 in the Richmond Hospital a long way from home, nor the admonition and prayer of the less-active sister, "Help us that we might love one another and overlook the tattoos." The words of the hymn by Susan Evans McCloud express my own feelings:

> *Savior, may I learn to love thee,*
> *Walk the path that thou hast shown,*
> *Pause to help and lift another,*
> *Finding strength beyond my own.*
> *Savior may I learn to love thee—*
> *Lord, I would follow thee.*
>
> *Who am I to judge another*
> *When I walk imperfectly?*
> *In the quiet heart is hidden*
> *Sorrow that the eye can't see.*
> *Who am I to judge another?*
> *Lord, I would follow thee.*
>
> *I would be my brother's keeper;*
> *I would learn the healer's art.*
> *To the wounded and the weary*
> *I would show a gentle heart.*
> *I would be my brother's keeper—*
> *Lord, I would follow thee.*
>
> *Savior, may I love my brother*
> *As I know thou lovest me,*
> *Find in thee my strength, my beacon,*
> *For thy servant I would be.*
> *Savior, may I love my brother—*
> *Lord, I would follow thee.*
>
> (*Hymns*, no. 220)

THE BLESSINGS
OF ADVERSITY

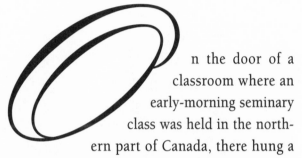O n the door of a classroom where an early-morning seminary class was held in the northern part of Canada, there hung a poster that caught my eye. In the picture a young boy is standing, frowning, under an umbrella with the rain beating down overhead. The caption reads, "I'll rise, but I won't shine."

We each can make that choice, you know. Sometimes we may not even want to rise, let alone shine. But what if, just *what if*, we could find the wherewithal to rise and shine every day? We would not be left to the whims of the rain or sun or circumstances to determine our attitude and the course of our days. We can rise and shine not just in the summer but in the spring, the fall, and even the wintertime in our lives when we understand the blessings of adversity.

The blessings of adversity usually come in such disguise that we would likely decline them if we could. But when we better understand the place of adversity, and even learn to be grateful

for this important part of our mortal experience, we will see that the experiences that drive us to extremity also bring us to Him who can and will succor us in all our infirmities (see Alma 7:12).

I think you will agree that if this profound doctrine, the great plan of happiness spoken of by Alma (see Alma 42:8), is to be understood, it requires more than the logic of man. From a strictly logical standpoint, much of mortality doesn't make sense, especially in times of affliction, tribulation, and sorrow. While many are losing faith and hope because of the adversities of our day, we can lift up our hearts and rejoice, even if we have just listened to the evening news.

Elder Dallin H. Oaks explained: "Our seeming downfalls can be a means of developing our strengths. Adversity will be a constant or occasional companion for each of us throughout our lives. We cannot avoid it. The only question is how we will react to it. Will our adversities be stumbling blocks or stepping stones?" (*BYU Devotional and Fireside Speeches, 1994–95* [Provo, Utah: Publication Graphics, 1995], p. 83).

I remember one period of time when I had some major responsibilities working with a group of people. Sometimes, when the weight of the load seemed too heavy and the obstacles insurmountable, I would say, "You just wait, this will turn to our good." I was often kidded about this. After some major disappointment on the way to our goal, someone would laughingly say, "Oh, we know: This will turn to our good." No one seemed very convinced. But now, looking back at the considerable evidence, we can see that it was always true.

I echo the prayer, "Oh God, I thank thee for answers to prayer. I thank thee for the times thou hast said no, and also for the times thou hast said yes. But I am even more aware of the many times thou hast said, 'Wait.' My heart overflows with gratitude for thy seeing direction for my good." We should live with expectation of some frustration, some adversity, some opposition. To accomplish the purposes of God, there must be "an opposition in all things" (2 Nephi 2:11).

President Spencer W. Kimball, who experienced so many severe trials in his life, wrote: "I am positive in my mind that the Lord has planned our destiny. Sometime we'll understand fully. And when we see back from the vantage point of the future, we shall be satisfied with many of the happenings of this life that are so difficult for us to comprehend" (*Faith Precedes the Miracle* [Salt Lake City: Deseret Book, 1972], p. 105).

It is helpful to have a few favorite scriptures and thoughts that we can turn to quickly when there seem to be no answers to the "why," on those days when we may be prone to deny the possibility that we even voted to sustain the plan. Here are some that I love:

Paul, suffering the persecution associated with his ministry, wrote: "We are troubled on every side, yet not distressed; we are perplexed, but not in despair; persecuted, but not forsaken; cast down, but not destroyed" (2 Corinthians 4:8–9). Does this suggest even the slightest indication of giving in or giving up? He continues in the spirit of a true disciple, "Our light affliction, which is but for a moment, worketh for us a far more exceeding and eternal weight of glory; while we look not at the things which are seen, but at the things which are not seen: for the things which are seen are temporal; but the things which are not seen are eternal" (2 Corinthians 4:17–18).

In the Book of Mormon, just before Alma's great discourse on faith, we read about his feelings for the people who were despised and cast out because of their poverty: "And now when Alma heard this, . . . he beheld with great joy; for he beheld that their afflictions had truly humbled them, and that they were in a preparation to hear the word" (Alma 32:6).

In a revelation given through Brigham Young at Winter Quarters, that very difficult time in the experience of the Saints, the Lord said: "My people must be tried in all things, that they may be prepared to receive the glory that I have for them, even the glory of Zion; and he that will not bear chastisement is not worthy of my kingdom" (D&C 136:31). After severe persecution suffered by the Saints in Missouri, the Lord gave them this promise, which is equally binding today: "Fear not, let your hearts be comforted; yea, rejoice evermore, and in everything give thanks; . . . all things wherewith you have been afflicted shall work together for your good" (D&C 98:1, 3).

Does he ask too much of us? Perhaps the size of our burden, the weight of our load, the intensity of our test may seem to be too great at times. Yet sometimes we fail to ask for his help to lighten our load because we are not sure our concern is big enough, given all the problems of the world. Of this I am sure: In our humble supplication, if something matters to us, it matters to the Lord.

What would you be willing to go through to make sure your spirit was in tune to receive personal revelation? The Prophet Joseph Smith taught, "Trials are at the very core of saintliness." In the words of C. S. Lewis, "Suffering is the megaphone God uses to get our attention."

With so much written about the need for adversity, one might ask how can we speak of the "great plan of *happiness*." It is in understanding that plan that we begin to see the blessings of adversity. The gospel of Jesus Christ literally changes lives. It brings light where there is darkness, hope where there is despair, faith in place of fear, and peace that passeth all understanding. When we come to understand the purpose of life, including the role of adversity and our relationship with our Lord and Savior Jesus Christ, then life takes on new meaning. We can trust in pending blessings that at first seem far removed. Instead of being consumed by our trials and tests, we're refined by them. Instead of losing our way, we find our way. We're drawn to the things of eternity while dealing with mortality.

Recently, when I was getting my hair cut, the young woman who was putting on the finishing touches remarked, in all seriousness, "I'll bet you were really pretty when you were young." (I would never have gone back to that salon except that she agreed to take the missionary discussions.) I bring this experience up not as an example of adversity but as a reminder that every one of us resides in what a friend of mine calls a "deteriorating body." Such evidences of the briefness of our mortal life help us see how essential it is to have a solid understanding of immortality.

I must tell you about my dear Aunt Alice, from whom I have learned some wonderful lessons. What a woman she is! She lives in Cardston and is now ninety-three years of age. If you were ever to see her when she was dressed up, you would find her wearing a perky little hat, a delicate chiffon scarf tied at her neck—"to cover the wrinkles," she says—a bright smile on her face, and a twinkle in her eye. A couple of years ago, her son took her to a Saturday night stake dance. This was a happy occasion, she was excited to report to me. She told me that several people had asked her to dance. Her excitement reminded me of a conversation I might have had with a girlfriend fifty years ago.

Following the dance she returned home, where she lives alone, exhausted but excited. She went to bed, but during the night she awakened. Her legs were swollen; her heart was pounding; she was afraid she was going to die. She explained to me that she felt she couldn't be found dead in bed looking like she did. So she got up and made her bed, changed into her nicest nightgown, put on fresh makeup, combed her hair, and went out to die on the living-room couch. She said she was quite surprised to awaken in the morning still alive.

Let me take you behind the scenes in this remarkable woman's life, that we might learn from her journey of blessings and adversity. She was asked to speak in stake conference in her ninetieth year, and she later sent me a handwritten copy of her message. With her permission, I share it with you:

> Our Savior's love is beyond comprehension. Sixty-three years ago, I became a wife. I thought that to be the most perfect love that ever could be. I hadn't enjoyed that love very long when my husband was called on a foreign mission, leaving me home to go through the tribulation of having our first baby alone. After he had been in the mission field about a month the baby was born. He became the center of my love and existence for two long years. When my husband returned, our lives were filled with love and thanksgiving for this adorable child. When he was five years old he was accidentally killed. It seemed all the light went out of the world for us. As I walked the streets at night unable to sleep, hoping to see that dear little face in a cloud somewhere, I came to love my Heavenly Father more as I pondered his words, "Take time to be still and know that I am God."

Some years later our beautiful Mark earned the money to put himself through his mission. Shortly before his release, I received a call from his mission president telling me that Mark was critically ill. He had cancer of the lungs. It seemed unbelievable. We had great faith that he would be healed through fasting and prayers, but it wasn't to be. Later in a dream I saw Mark walking towards me with a beautiful smile on his face and his arms outstretched to embrace me. I awoke happy and content once again that my son, Mark, lived where his life was one of sublime quality of love.

She goes on to mention that when Mark was just a baby, their family life was anything but ideal. She doesn't say any more about the details, but I will add that her husband had become addicted to alcohol and all the related tragedies that go with that terrible disease. Concerning that time, she writes:

As I put my dear baby down for the night and the two older children were gone to bed, I dropped on my knees by the couch and poured out my heart to Heavenly Father as I had never done before. I thought my heart would break with the sorrow that possessed me. I said, "Father, if things can't change, if I only knew that my prayer was heard, then with the love that I have for these dear children, we will survive some way." In my prayer, I had wondered how Father could let me know.

The next day was fast and testimony meeting. I said I would try to bear my testimony, which I wasn't in the habit of doing, and perhaps he would let me know in that way. While I bowed there in humble prayer, a warm, wonderful feeling enveloped me—that sweet peace that passeth all understanding. And although I didn't see anyone, I knew there was a holy presence there. It was so strong I was unable to arise for a

short time. I knew my prayer was heard, but I went to testimony meeting determined to bear my testimony as I had said, although I didn't need any more assurance. At the beginning of the meeting the bishop arose and said he would like to hear Sister Alice bear her testimony in song. How I ever got to my feet or what I said I will never remember as I received that second assurance that my prayer was heard.

The love of music has ever been a moving force of enjoyment. As I was called upon to sing that lovely song, "I Walked Today Where Jesus Walked," the thought came to me, I most likely would never walk where Jesus walked in this life, but I knew I had walked and felt his presence here. I had never knelt in the Garden of Gethsemane where all alone he prayed. But I knew I had knelt and prayed and I wasn't alone. Some divine presence was there. I was able to pick my heavy burden up and, with him by my side, I climbed the hill of Calvary where on the cross he died for my sins and yours. My heavy burden was gone and I lived. I lived as I had never experienced life before. A sweet peace filled my soul and, as the love for my Savior grew, I recalled the words in John 17:3, "And this is life eternal, that they might know thee the only true God, and Jesus Christ, whom thou hast sent."

We know *about* our Savior, but it is often in our adversities that we truly find him and know him and love him. In our times of trial, if we will turn to him, the Spirit bears witness that our Savior not only can but will ease our burdens.

In this mortal life of trials and tests, no one is spared the refining fire of adversity. President Spencer W. Kimball, whose life was fraught with physical struggles in a long series of medical challenges, spoke of his gratitude for adversity through a poem he liked to quote:

Pain stayed so long I said to him today,
"I will not have you with me any more."
I stamped my foot and said, "Be on your way,"
And paused there, startled at the look he wore.
"I, who have been your friend," he said to me.
"I, who have been your teacher—all you know
Of understanding love, of sympathy,
And patience, I have taught you. Shall I go?"
He spoke the truth, this strange unwelcome guest;
I watched him leave, and knew that he was wise.
He left a heart grown tender in my breast,
He left a far, clear vision in my eyes.
I dried my tears, and lifted up a song—
Even for one who'd tortured me so long.

> (Author unknown; quoted in Spencer W. Kimball, *Faith
> Precedes the Miracle*, p. 99)

Through the writings of Orson F. Whitney we are reminded:

No pain that we suffer, no trial that we experience is wasted. It ministers to our education, to the development of such qualities as patience, faith, fortitude and humility. All that we suffer and all that we endure, especially when we endure it patiently, builds up our characters, purifies our hearts, expands our souls, and makes us more tender and charitable, more worthy to be called the children of God . . . and it is through sorrow and suffering, toil and tribulation, that we gain the education that we come here to acquire and which will make us more like our Father and Mother in heaven. (As quoted by Adney Y. Komatsu, *Ensign*, May 1987, p. 79)

This life experience is designed for our growth and progress. Our trials will not be more than we can handle, but they cannot be less if we are to fill the measure of our creation. Some of our afflictions may be a result of disobedience and could be avoided by keeping the commandments. Some are the result of error and others the consequence of sin. Some are simply the effects of mortality. Whatever the case, the Lord has said, "Come unto me, and I will heal you." This healing can be physical, spiritual, or emotional—whatever is needful—and it will come in his own way, not always on our time line but ever at the right time. In a profound message from President Howard W. Hunter, we hear his gentle, powerful plea: "To those who have transgressed or been offended, we say, come back. To those who are hurt and struggling and afraid, we say, let us stand with you and dry your tears. To those who are confused and assailed by error on every side, we say, come to the God of all truth and the Church of continuing revelation. Come back. Stand with us. Carry on. Be believing. All is well, and all will be well. . . . Have hope, exert faith, receive—and give—charity, the pure love of Christ" (*Ensign,* July 1994, p. 5).

Our Lord and Savior Jesus Christ, who marked the path and led the way, extends the invitation, "Come, follow me." We read in Hebrews 5:8, "Though he were a Son, yet learned he obedience by the things which he suffered." Yes, we are to suffer, and as we read from Alma 7:12 we better understand why the Savior is able to understand not only our struggles and our afflictions but also our feelings: "And he will take upon him death, that he may loose the bands of death which bind his people; and he will take upon him their infirmities, that his bowels may be filled with mercy, according to the flesh, that he may know according to the flesh how to succor his people according to their infirmities" (Alma 7:12).

Can we tell him anything about struggle or suffering that he does not know and understand—anything about loneliness, about rejection, about abuse? Do you think he understands about sorrow? And though he was without sin himself, do you think he knows of the consequence of sin, when he voluntarily took upon himself the weight of all our sins and transgressions? If we choose to follow him, he will be with us even in the fiery furnace.

BE OF GOOD COMFORT

*I*t has been said that you must have a hook on your line if you want to catch a fish. Our questions are like hooks on our lines. They prepare us to receive.

With this in mind, let us consider the story of Alma and his people being persecuted by Amulon. We read: "And it came to pass that the voice of the Lord came to them in their afflictions, saying: Lift up your heads and be of good comfort, for I know of the covenant which ye have made unto me; and I will covenant with my people and deliver them out of bondage. And I will also ease the burdens which are put upon your shoulders, that even you cannot feel them upon your backs, even while you are in bondage; and this will I do that ye may stand as witnesses for me hereafter, and that ye may know of a surety that I, the Lord God, do visit my people in their afflictions" (Mosiah 24:13–14).

And now we might ask the following questions, preparing our minds to receive comfort for our time and season as we liken these scriptures unto ourselves. Are we in bondage today? What are our afflictions? What does the Lord mean when he says he will ease the burdens on our backs? Which burdens? All of them? How? When? What is our part in our covenant relationship with the Lord that must be in place so that he can keep his promise as he desires?

About fifty years ago Richard L. Evans wrote: "At the moment of our greatest achievements we are on the brink of the most unspeakable horrors." This statement might well have been written at the time the Saints left Kirtland, or Nauvoo, or Winter Quarters. It seems just as relevant today. However, in every season, even "on the brink of the most unspeakable horrors," the Lord's promise stands: "I will ease the burdens which are put upon your shoulders."

The experiences of the early Saints bear poignant testimony of that promise. As a reminder of the burdens and the sacrifice of those stalwart people, I share a brief excerpt from my own family's history:

> It was 1846. Others who arrived at Mt. Pisgah made their camp on another part of the mountain from where my great-great-grandmother Susan Kent Greene's tent was located. She was far from neighbors. Almost as soon as Evan, her husband, had left her to go back and help others, their baby, a beautiful girl of eleven months, became ill. The baby rapidly grew worse and after a few days died in its mother's arms. This occurred on a dark, stormy night. The storm was accompanied by loud thunderbolts and vivid lightning flashes, which would have struck terror to the heart of a lone woman even if she had been in favorable circumstances, if she were at all frightened of those things. The oldest child and only boy in the family at that time was but eight years of age, and Susan did not dare send him out alone to seek help. All she could

do was to pray that the Lord would not forsake her but would send someone to help.

About ten o'clock that night a young man came to the door of the tent. The young man spoke words of pity and comfort and sat watching Susan through the night. In the morning he made a coffin and dug a grave for the baby and buried it. Susan had to prepare the little body for its last rest herself.

Such trials and afflictions we can hardly imagine, and yet throughout her journal Susan wrote of the peace and the comfort that were always present, of her knowledge that the Lord would never abandon them. On February 3, 1875, at the age of fifty-one, she wrote: "I make this covenant to do the very best I can, asking God for wisdom to direct me that I may walk with him in all righteousness and truth. I much desire to be pure in heart that I may see God. Help me Lord to overcome all evil with good. This covenant with the writings on this page is written with my blood and I have not broken my covenant and trust I shall not. (Signed) Susan K. Greene."

I have asked myself again and again, how did those mothers and fathers and children carry the burdens upon their backs? They suffered through cold and heat, hunger and disease. They were driven from their homes—even their temporary homes—persecuted and wounded. They buried loved ones in shallow graves along the way and with faith in God sang, "And should we die before our journey's through, Happy day! All is well!" (*Hymns,* no. 30). All their actions testified of their faith that although the physical body may be taken home, the righteous have no need to fear—all is well.

Theirs was a test of physical endurance that we can hardly comprehend. How did they walk with faith in every footstep until eventually they reached the Great Salt Lake Valley? How did they decide what they would make room for in their wagons and what they would leave behind? Can you hear the discussion? "How can I bear to leave my piano?" says the mother. The child cries, clinging to her doll, "I don't want to go if I can't take my dolls and toys and the little cupboard with my dishes." "What about Grandma's chest that she brought from Denmark?" If they tried to take everything they loved, they would get mired down in the mud on the trail while others moved on.

Today we are pioneers on a new frontier. Our burdens are different, but I am convinced that it is equally important today, maybe even more so, that we decide what we will make room for in our wagons. What will we take with us, and what will we be willing to sacrifice in order to avoid getting mired down in the mud of today?

The early pioneers' burden was largely of a physical nature. Ours is different. We will not need to unload a favorite heirloom, a rocker, a piano along the trail to lighten the load. We carry many of our burdens not in wagons but in our minds, in our thoughts, and in our hearts. We must discard burdens of pride, envy, jealousy, resentment, anger, fear, and negative thoughts of self-deprecation, discouragement, and despair.

Our pioneer forefathers fought the terrible plague of crickets that came to destroy their crops. Men, women, and children prayed and fought these ravaging crickets in a desperate effort to save their fields. The Lord heard their earnest prayers and sent seagulls, which devoured the crickets and miraculously saved the crops.

The crickets of our day are different from those in times past. They are more powerful, more dangerous, and less recognizable.

At first things may appear to be very innocent; thoughts, words, and pictures are placed into our minds in subtle and sophisticated ways. If we are not watchful, the crickets will creep into our safe places: our homes, our hearts, our minds. Through television, radio, magazines, movies, literature, music, and fashions, these evil influences will aggressively begin their silent destruction, multiplying their forces as they go and attacking and destroying our spiritual growth.

Thoughts of self-deprecation and inferiority can be like black crickets relentlessly working to erode the foundation, the fiber of our faith. Just as the Lord sent the seagulls to destroy the crickets for the early Saints, he has provided safety and protection for us in the form of covenants and blessings to enhance our spirituality. When we have the Lord's spirit with us, we will not be deceived by the evil influences of the world. Every right choice can conquer a cricket and lighten the load.

In the Doctrine and Covenants we read, "And inasmuch as they erred it might be made known; and inasmuch as they sought wisdom they might be instructed; and inasmuch as they sinned they might be chastened, that they might repent; and inasmuch as they were humble they might be made strong, and blessed from on high, and receive knowledge from time to time" (D&C 1:25–28). Does that sound as if the Lord knew we were going to make mistakes? We must avoid the self-imposed burden of excessive guilt over the minor infractions that are a part of our mortal experience as we learn to walk by faith.

In the mission field, occasionally a young elder or sister would do something that reflected his or her youth and inexperience and poor judgment. My husband, with a stern look but a twinkle in his eye, would say, "You act like you're nineteen or twenty," and then add, "but it is to your advantage that I am a senior citizen and I don't remember very well."

We have lessons to learn every step of the journey, at every age and stage. We will always be contending with the gap between our desired perfection and the reality of our daily lives. This was brought to my mind vividly one day when my husband had been up early in the morning trimming the roses, mowing the lawn, emptying the garbage, and so on. I had also been busily engaged with my own list of things to get accomplished for that day. About ten o'clock in the morning, I heard a knock on the window and looked up to see my husband standing there with a large piece of cardboard on which he had printed: "Will work for food." I opened the door and invited him in, suggesting that he might wish to fix breakfast for both of us. We laughed together even while I winced at how far I had strayed from my original intent to be the perfect wife. My point is this: Although serving breakfast on time may be a desirable goal, it is not one of eternal consequence. Feeling guilt over all our little shortcomings is a burden that can distract us from our larger purpose.

Today we live in a state of emergency, not necessarily in a physical sense but certainly in a spiritual one. These are the days spoken of in Paul's writings to Timothy: "This know also, that in the last days perilous times shall come. For men shall be lovers of their own selves, covetous, boasters, proud, blasphemers, disobedient to parents, unthankful, unholy, without natural affection, trucebreakers, false accusers, incontinent, fierce, despisers of those that are good" (2 Timothy 3:1–3). A headline in a newspaper reporting President Gordon B. Hinckley's address at the Provo Community Centennial Fireside stated, "Prophet Laments Social Illness." President Hinckley said on that occasion: "I am more concerned about the growing moral deficit in the nation than I am about the monetary deficit. . . . We are shutting the doors of our homes against the God of the universe. Divine law has become a meaningless phrase. What was once spoken of as sin is now referred to as only poor judgment. Transgression has been placed by misbehavior." What is the answer? President Hinckley responds, "People who carry in their hearts a strong conviction concerning the living reality of the Almighty and of accountability to him for what we do with our lives and our society are far less likely to become enmeshed in those problems which inevitably weaken our society."

We stand on the threshold of a new frontier, facing the crickets, the challenges of our day. Does our spiritual preparation seem as important to our survival as was our ancestors' physical preparation? And if we do our part in preparation, what might we expect? In the case of Alma and his brethren who were in bondage, "The voice of the Lord came to them in their afflictions" (Mosiah 24:13). Whenever we are weighed down with concerns that keep us from the spirit of the Lord, we are in a real sense in bondage, burdened with a load that keeps us from progressing as we might. May the voice of the Lord attend us in our afflictions, helping us know what to make room for and what to discard from our wagons. As we learn to walk with faith in every footstep, we too will feel the burdens ease from our shoulders, and we will take comfort in the sure knowledge that the Lord fulfills his promises.

A PERFECT
BRIGHTNESS OF HOPE

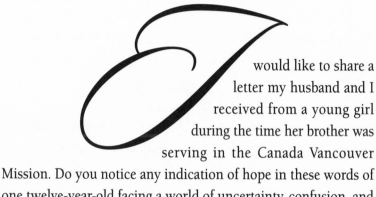 would like to share a letter my husband and I received from a young girl during the time her brother was serving in the Canada Vancouver Mission. Do you notice any indication of hope in these words of one twelve-year-old facing a world of uncertainty, confusion, and disillusionment?

Dear President and Sister Kapp,

This is Becky. I just want to tell you a bit about myself and ask some questions. Well, first of all, I'm twelve years old. I'll be thirteen November 1st. I play the piano and flute. I also sing and run track. I get good grades in school. Now, don't get me wrong, I'm not trying to brag. I'm just informing you of what my talents are. Besides, I wouldn't have any of these if it weren't for Heavenly Father. Oh, and I love to write. One time I wrote on my hero. Guess who that was? Jesus Christ. I got second place on that one. No matter what the judges thought I knew that paper was tops.

Now, I hope you are not too busy because I'd like to write to you. You see, I have got a plan. After I get married in the Salt Lake City Temple my husband and I will live just outside of a large, busy city suburb in the nice country where there are beautiful mountains, flowers, woods and maybe a stream. While my husband works I'll be home cooking, taking care of our children and writing. My husband will bring in most of the money except when I get a book published and he'll have long vacations so we can spend time with the kids. It'll be great. I'll write children's books and maybe a novel here and there.

As you can see, I can go on forever talking about all sorts of things. I'll write again and talk with you some more. 'Bye now.

Love, Becky

Does Becky realize there is a mean world out there filled with disappointment, despair, discouragement, sin, and suffering? Should I have written back and told her how it really is: that not every dream is fulfilled and not every prayer is answered exactly as we may wish? Should we dash hope before it gets out of hand and leads us into paths that may not be realistic or rational?

Of course not! Hope is a gift from God that comes to us by and through the Holy Ghost. All this is reflected in our attitude about life, our vision of possibilities. Hope is future oriented. It allows us to live in anticipation, to get up in the morning expecting a good day. And if that good day doesn't materialize, hope helps us to realize that there is always a tomorrow. As the lead character in the delightful play *Annie* sings—always at the top of her lungs—"The sun will come out tomorrow."

I know something about hoping, month after month, year after year, for answers that seem ever delayed and desires deferred. So do you. The customized curriculum, I believe, is for our growth. And hope is a powerful, sustaining, even exhilarating feeling that can uphold us while we anticipate the possibilities not yet realized. Hope is like tiny seeds hidden deep beneath the ground, planted in fertile soil of faith and nourished through feasting on the words of Christ, praying fervently, repenting daily, forgiving eagerly, and meditating frequently. The result is an abundant harvest that, like wheat stored in bins, provides sustenance through winter seasons.

Consider the words of Nephi, admonishing us to keep the glow, the warmth, the radiation of the Spirit ever emanating from us, even in a darkening and dismal world. Speaking to those who have accepted the covenants of baptism, he says:

> And now, my beloved brethren, after ye have gotten into this strait and narrow path, I would ask if all is done? Behold, I say unto you, Nay; for ye have not come thus far save it were by the word of Christ with unshaken faith in him, relying wholly upon the merits of him who is mighty to save. Wherefore, ye must press forward with a steadfastness in Christ, having a perfect brightness of hope, and a love of God and of all men. Wherefore, if ye shall press forward, feasting upon the word of Christ, and endure to the end, behold, thus saith the Father: Ye shall have eternal life. And now, behold, my beloved brethren, this is the way; and there is none other way nor name given under heaven whereby man can be saved in the kingdom of God. (2 Nephi 31:19–21)

This perfect brightness of hope is not to be reserved only for when the sun is shining in our lives and things are going well. Even in times of trial, we can sing, "There is hope smiling brightly before us, and we know that deliv'rance is nigh" (*Hymns*, no. 19). All of us have hopes, "high, apple pie, in the sky hopes," as the old song declares. Some hope the doctor will announce, "Not malignant." Some hope the employer will say, "You're hired." Some hope the report will read, "You're pregnant." Some hope the Lord will say, "You're forgiven." Hope drives us around the next corner, over the next hill, through the hot sun and the cold winter.

I have sitting on the shelf in my closet an old, worn-out pair of men's shoes. They are priceless; you couldn't purchase a pair like them, and these are not for sale. They are probably about a size 10 and a D width, I would guess, and have a good shine on the top. They once belonged to a young man who served a mission for the Lord, but for now they are mine. He gave them to me. I wish you could see him in your mind's eye as I see him, but I'm sure when I tell you the story you will have someone come to mind who will fit these shoes.

Upon our arrival in the mission field, we quietly asked several individuals, "Who do you think are the extra-mile missionaries?" Although several different names were given, without exception this young man whose shoes I have would always be mentioned. You can be sure we were anxious to meet him.

In just a day or two we met this young elder. He was a fine-looking young man, but not particularly outgoing or dynamic, as one might suppose. When we learned more about him, we became aware that things had not always turned out the way he had hoped. He had perhaps not participated in as many baptisms, not always had totally obedient companions, and not always experienced the sunshiny days he might have hoped for; in fact, there seemed to be a lot of rain in his life.

There are many, many disappointments that go with

missionary work and with life, but this young man always seemed to have a vision of what could be. He worked with a hope that was relentless. His hope allowed him to see more than others could see. He was always well-groomed and happy, and even though it was near the end of his mission, when even the best-cared-for white shirts begin to show signs of many washings, he still looked good and his shoes were always shined.

One day he was in the office writing a quick note, kneeling by a desk because no chair was immediately available. I walked into the room and my eyes became riveted on the soles of his shoes. "Elder," I said, "tell me about your shoes." He smiled and stood up quickly, covering the evidence of his worn-out soles. "What are you going to do with those shoes when you return home?" I asked him. With a big smile, he told me he was going to trash them. He saw no value in them. They were completely worn out; even the cardboard that had been used to cover the large holes in the bottoms was worn through.

Yes, they were thoroughly worn out, but to me their value was far greater than it had been when they were new. "Elder," I asked, "will you give me your shoes?" He looked quite surprised, but agreed that I could have his shoes with the soles that had been worn through in the sacred labor of saving souls. He asked me what I intended to do with them, and I told him I was going to keep them and in twenty years or so, if I was still around, I was going to present them to his son or daughter who would be filling a mission and say to him or her, "Walk in the steps of your noble father."

About two years later, in one of the last zone conferences we held before we finished our mission, I used those shoes as a visual aid. Many of the young missionaries had their eyes fill with tears when I spoke of giving the shoes to that young man's children as a reminder to walk in their father's footsteps. After relating the story, I saw one young elder, revealing the evidence of a tender heart, brush away a tear from his eye. Then, as if to cover the evidence, he smiled and whispered to his companion, "Maybe they were cheap shoes." With that smile I saw renewed hope and commitment, determination and dedication. In spite of the slammed doors, the rainy days, the discouragement, the disappointments, and sometimes the despair, still that spark of hope never dies.

We too have been invited to walk in our Father's footsteps. We don't have his shoes, but we do have his well-marked path. "Therefore being justified by faith, we have peace with God through our Lord Jesus Christ: by whom also we have access by faith into this grace wherein we stand, and rejoice in hope of the glory of God. . . . And hope maketh not ashamed; because the love of God is shed abroad in our hearts by the Holy Ghost which is given unto us" (Romans 5:1–2, 5).

Hope falls like gentle rain, one drop at a time, into a reservoir made ready through feasting and fasting, praying and meditating, repenting and forgiving and serving. Continuous replenishment is essential if the reservoir is to be a resource that can be drawn from in times of spiritual drought. Let us press forward with a perfect brightness of hope and claim the promise of the Lord, "Ye shall have eternal life" (2 Nephi 31:20).

MASTER,
THE TEMPEST IS RAGING

J learned as a child to observe carefully the looks on my parents' faces as they stood on the edge of our eighty-acre field of grain and watched dark clouds gathering in the north. When the tender shoots of grain had barely broken through the heavy soil, and the financial welfare of our family was at stake, I learned something of the dangerous, destructive forces of a heavy rainstorm. I sensed the helplessness, the anxiety, and the urgency with which my parents would stand in the open field, study the clouds, and look at the tender shoots and then each other. On some occasions, they would drop to their knees in prayer. As the sky darkened and the wind began to blow, the questions pounded in my heart: Would the crops survive? Would there be a harvest? Would there be money to pay the bank for the seeds that had been sown in faith?

I learned that there are different kinds of storm clouds in different seasons. "It's hail," Dad said on one occasion, removing his hat and wiping his brow with the sleeve of his shirt. "Those are hail clouds," he explained as he surveyed with some anxiety our large flock of young turkeys, the hope of our future. I stood at his side reading his countenance to determine the seriousness of the situation. We went to the barn, closed the gate, put things away, and hurried for the house just as the small hailstones began to drop from the darkened sky. We stood at the window and watched. The sounds of the hail confirmed the size of the pellets; this was no ordinary storm. We watched, waited, and prayed.

By morning the storm had passed, but it left devastating reminders of its destructive force. Our young turkeys, in which we had placed such hope, were dead—more than a hundred of them, lying on the ground where they had been hit by the hail. Crop failure, we called it. Crop failure.

I am still stirred with some anxiety by dark clouds and the threat of storms that can wipe out tender shoots and kill young birds. But I am even more concerned with storms raging today that are not the kind you can close the doors or lock the windows against. Worldly hail beats on us over the airwaves, through the media, and from the marketplace. How can we survive such tempests? The scriptures contain several accounts of severe storms; valuable lessons in survival can be found in those stories.

One such storm, on the Sea of Galilee, was made more real to me by an experience I had some years ago when my husband and I went with a group of friends to the Holy Land. We were all full of anticipation, excited to walk where Jesus walked and feel his presence there. Our first stop was at the Sea of Galilee. I stood breathless on the shore. In my mind's eye I could see the ship with the disciples aboard. There were waves on the water, and the wind was blowing. I wondered just how long Peter's faith had allowed him to walk on the water before he began to sink (see Matthew 14:24–33). I felt as though I were reliving the experience in every detail.

That first evening, we held a sacrament service on the shore of the Sea of Galilee. I listened again, more with my heart than with my mind, to what it means to take upon us his name and to keep his commandments so we can have his Spirit to be with us.

The following day there was actually a storm on the Sea of Galilee. There were no boats on the water, but we were able to persuade a guide to take us out in spite of the threatening storm, since this would be our only chance to actually be on the Sea of Galilee.

Out some distance from shore the wind gradually increased until there was a real storm, and the ship was being tossed to and fro. Our guide stood at the helm gripping the mast, the wind whipping his clothing. We all held our jackets tight around us and struggled to keep our scriptures open so we could follow along as our guide read to us, shouting through the storm. The pages from the scriptures that I took to the Holy Land with me are still marked with the wind and the storm from that occasion—water from the Sea of Galilee.

Even yet, when I open those scriptures, I can hear the voice of our guide through the wind: "But straightway Jesus spake unto them, saying, Be of good cheer; it is I; be not afraid. And Peter answered him and said, Lord, if it be thou, bid me come unto thee on the water. And he said, Come. And when Peter was come down out of the ship, he walked on the water, to go to Jesus. But when he saw the wind boisterous, he was afraid; and beginning to sink, he cried, saying, Lord, save me. And immediately Jesus stretched forth his hand, and caught him, and said unto him, O thou of little faith, wherefore didst thou doubt?" (Matthew 14:27–31).

It is possible that none of us in this earth life will have the faith to walk on the water. But if our choices are right, we can be in the boat. When the wind is boisterous and we are afraid and beginning to sink and we cry out, "Lord, save me," it is as though Jesus stretches out his hands to us and invites us to come aboard the ship. Then our wind will cease and there will be peace, and hopefully we will call through the storm to others and say, "We have found him. We have found him. Come and see."

The scriptures abound with accounts of storms. How important was it to Noah and his family that he received and followed the guidelines, the promptings of the Spirit, on how to build an ark that would provide protection from the storm? Did it matter to Nephi's family, even his rebellious brothers, that he was able to construct a ship after the manner shown him by the Lord? Indeed, his faith was so strong that he quieted the resistance of his brothers with these words, "If God had commanded me to do all things I could do them" (1 Nephi 17:50). Did it matter that the brother of Jared and his family received instructions on the procedure for building barges—eight of them—that might survive the storm? I believe the Lord is saying to each of us today, "Ask. Ask how to build an ark, a ship, a barge, a safe place to protect your family in times of storm. Listen, and I will give you instructions on how to survive. I have in the past; I will again, and again."

Today to secure our arks, our homes, our safe places, we put deadbolts on the doors, motion-sensor lights in the yard, burglar alarms in the entrances, smoke detectors in every room, double-paned glass in the windows, and insulation and weather stripping around all the openings. We kneel down and pray, asking to be protected from harm or accident and from the powers of the adversary. And then, too often, we get up, turn on the TV or the videos or the music, grab a quick bite from the microwave, and go to our separate rooms without really talking. In the lonely noise of our homes, we are under attack.

In times of war (a real storm), the enemy's first effort is focused on destroying the communication center. In families as well as in nations, when the communication breaks down, the war rages. Satan's effective strategy is to do everything possible to stop our communication and to separate us, if not physically, then emotionally and spiritually. If possible, his plans would have us eating, but not together; praying, but not together; living in the same house, but apart. When parents and youth are isolated and insulated from each other by the lack of communication, there is danger in our homes. We can be out of touch even when we are within reach.

When the Lord saw fit to chasten the wicked who were building the Tower of Babel, he confounded their language. He stopped their communication. We have a blueprint for survival from the example of the brother of Jared and his family. First we read that the brother of Jared cried unto the Lord that he and his brother would be able to understand each other (see Ether 1:35). The Lord responded. Then the brother of Jared made a second request, that they and their friends could be in touch, not be confounded. The Lord also granted this request. This communication opened up many possibilities.

Having received such positive responses so far, Jared pressed his brother further, "Go and inquire of the Lord whether he will drive us out of the land, . . . and who knoweth but the Lord will carry us forth into a land which is choice above all the earth" (Ether 1:38). The message got through, and an answer was given of the Lord: "I will go before thee into a land which is choice above all the lands of the earth" (Ether 1:42). Jared and his brothers followed the counsel, the blueprints. They built barges according to the instructions of the Lord.

After following the instructions, including preparing the food and water, gathering the flocks and herds, and getting everyone on board, they were ready, and we read that they "set forth into the sea, commending themselves unto the Lord their God" (Ether 6:4). They were prepared; they were ready physically. But before the storm ended and they reached their destination, they would have greater opportunities for continued spiritual growth.

Now, wouldn't it seem that after such a demonstration of faith and obedience, including the brother of Jared's personal sacred experience with the Lord, they would have smooth sailing? Let us follow their journey. The account begins: "The Lord God caused that there should be a furious wind blow upon the face of the waters, . . . and they were many times buried in the depths of the sea" (Ether 6:5–6). It must have been terribly frightening, and yet, "When they were buried in the deep there was no water that could hurt them, their vessels being tight like unto a dish, and also they were tight like unto the ark of Noah; therefore when they were encompassed about by many waters they did cry unto the Lord, and he did bring them forth again upon the top of the waters. And it came to pass that the wind did never cease to blow . . . " (Ether 6:7–8). But note that it never did cease to blow "*towards the promised land*" (Ether 6:8; emphasis added). They were driven forth before the wind toward their goal. Once they understood the purpose for the wind and knowing that their vessels were tight, we read further, "And they did sing praises unto the Lord. . . . And when they had set their feet upon the shores of the promised land they bowed themselves down upon the face of the land, and did humble themselves before the Lord, and did shed tears of joy before the Lord, because of the multitude of his tender mercies over them" (Ether 6:9, 12).

I have come to realize that storms can destroy, but they can also save us if we are prepared. It may well be that the wind and the storms in our life provide the thrust to push us onward and upward to our promised land.

In all the storms that we have discussed, there seems to be a common factor for those who would survive: They must get on the boat. Whether we are constructing a barge, an ark, or some other place of safety, we must follow the Lord's instructions and prepare ourselves for the storm.

For three years, while serving in the Canada Vancouver Mission, every month Heber and I would board the *Spirit of Columbia* ferry to Victoria on Vancouver Island. There was seldom ever a concern for storms that might endanger our safety, but there was another problem. Because of the excessive tourist travel, especially during the summer months, people might go an hour or more early and sit in their cars waiting in line for tickets to board. Although the ferry would hold 2,000 passengers, 470 cars and trucks, still during those busy times it would often pull out with many, many eager travelers left behind. If we missed the boat, we would leave our missionaries stranded, some

of them having traveled more than two hours from opposite ends of the island for zone conference.

This possibility of missing the ferry was a major concern to us—until one day we were introduced to a system called the "assured loading plan." Well in advance of your journey you could purchase, if you could pay the price, a small packet of ten tickets. On the back of each ticket were the words: "This voucher may be presented by the purchaser in payment of one passenger vehicle up to six feet, eight inches, in height and driver fare for ferry service between Vancouver Island to the lower mainland in accordance with the current tariff. Non-transferable. One ticket per sailing." Fortunately, we had the resources to purchase the assured loading tickets to be used in an emergency. We could see how this could be a tremendous advantage to us. We would always be assured of being on the boat—with the added benefit that with an assured loading ticket we would be directed along the ramp to the upper deck, the more desirable position for the trip.

Our Father in Heaven has a plan to assure that we will reach our destination on the top deck, so to speak. We can carry an "assured loading pass," a temple recommend, and know that it gives evidence of the covenants we have made. We need to have the spiritual resources to qualify us for the recommend. If we would be on board, we must set aside the things of the world that would tear us apart, and focus on the things of eternity that keep us fixed in our purpose, riveted on the stars that guide us safely home.

Yes, we can join in acknowledging that the tempest is raging, the billows are tossing high. Obedience to the commandments of God assures our safe travel. Without the commandments, we lose the light of Christ. In every stage and every age we have an opportunity to declare our position, whether we will miss the boat or be on board safe with the Master at the helm. If we choose to come unto Christ, he promises peace and comfort, even in times of storm:

> *When through the deep waters I call thee to go,*
> *The rivers of sorrow shall not thee o'erflow,*
> *For I will be with thee, thy troubles to bless,*
> *And sanctify to thee thy deepest distress.*
>
> (*Hymns*, no. 85)

EARS TO HEAR

As a young man in the U.S. Navy, my husband was stationed on a ship. His position as a signalman was next to the huge artillery guns, which were fired frequently. This was the beginning of a deterioration in his hearing that has accelerated over the years. Today, without the benefit of hearing aids with a large amplifier in each ear, he is almost totally deaf. I can stand very close and shout, and if he has not yet put in his hearing aids in the morning, he hears nothing. My niece, Shelly, asked me one time, "How do you whisper sweet nothings to him?" "Like this," I said, putting my hands to my mouth. "I shout, 'I love you,' and he can read my lips."

There are problems associated with hearing aids. In the car, the road noise is very distracting. In the office, the noise of the machines, especially copiers and fluorescent lights, becomes amplified. In a restaurant, the clatter of dishes or music; in the chapel, the air conditioning—it seems that mechanical sounds always drown out the human voice, even if people are sitting side by side. And in a group it is very difficult to distinguish one voice from another.

Still, his hearing loss caused no major difficulty in our lives until one occasion not too long ago. We were away from home on an assignment when the batteries in his hearing aids died, and we did not have any extra batteries with us. Heber still had the hearing aids in each ear, but they were of no value without the batteries. As we drove along the highway, I could speak to him, but he could not hear; he could speak to me, but I could not answer him. There was no verbal communication. We were together, but nothing was getting through. We rode in silence, side by side. Can you imagine what an anxious feeling of isolation that is? What if we could never talk to each other or hear each other the way we were used to?

Fortunately, the problem was easily resolved. The minute we could get to the store and purchase those tiny batteries, we were joyfully in touch again. Imagine how different our lives would be without the batteries, even though he had the hearing aids and we were side by side.

A scripture in the Doctrine and Covenants invites us to "give ear to the voice of the living God" (D&C 50:1). The voice of the Spirit, like the hearing aid, is available to us but can function only if our battery is charged. The Lord said, "The Spirit enlighteneth every man [and every woman] . . . that hearkeneth to the voice of the Spirit" (D&C 84:46). He also said, "Every one that hearkeneth to the voice of the Spirit cometh unto God, even the Father" (D&C 84:47). The question is never whether God is speaking to us, but rather, can we hear? Are we hearkening to the voice of the Spirit? Just as there are many mechanical sounds that drown out the human voice, so the adversary will use every conceivable method to create road noise along the highway of life in an effort to drown out the voice of the Spirit.

I believe that in a very real way our Father in Heaven is shouting to each of us, "I love you." But our batteries may be dead, and though he is near, the message does not get through and there is instead a terrible feeling of isolation and loneliness and sometimes even despair. When our batteries are not charged, we're deprived of the workings of the Spirit. The Holy Ghost is a comforter, a teacher, and when we are filled with the Spirit we can hear.

At a mission presidents seminar in 1975, President Ezra Taft Benson said, "The Spirit is the most important matter in this glorious work." Although the Spirit is essential if the message is to get through, some of us may not know how it functions. Parley P. Pratt wrote of the workings of the Spirit:

> The gift of the Holy Ghost . . . quickens all the intellectual faculties, increases, enlarges, expands, and purifies all the natural passions and affections, and adapts them, by the gift of wisdom, to their lawful use. It inspires, develops, cultivates, and matures all the fine-toned sympathies, joys, tastes, kindred feelings, and affections of our nature. It inspires virtue, kindness, goodness, tenderness, gentleness, and charity. It develops beauty of person, form, and feature. It tends to health, vigor, animation, and social feeling. It invigorates all the faculties of the physical and intellectual man. It strengthens and gives tone to the nerves. In short, it is, as it were, marrow to the bone, joy to the heart, light to the eyes, music to the ears, and life to the whole being. (*Key to the Science of Theology* [Salt Lake City: Deseret Book, 1978], p. 61)

That is what we can experience if our batteries are charged. Could there ever be a possibility that we would receive such a wonderful gift and never unwrap it, never use it, never hear it, never enjoy the blessings for which it was given?

It is not always easy to follow the promptings of the Spirit, but if we keep our batteries charged and have ears to hear, we will be guided. May I share with you a letter that I received from a young woman, a seminary teacher whom I had the privilege of supervising as a student teacher years ago at Brigham Young University. She writes:

> I signed up to teach another year of seminary. It will be my fourth year. It is so incredibly hard and incredibly wonderful all at the same time. You get up at 5 A.M. and cry when the alarm goes off because you are so tired from being up all night helping with a school project or something. You grope in the dark for shoes and almost leave with a blue and a black one on. The profound thought you had the day before as you studied Alma is gone, as is all remembrance of any portion of the lesson. You lock your keys in the car with the ignition running when you get out to take off the chain to the church parking lot in the dark. Once again you plead with the Lord to help you teach, as you know it is way beyond your capacity and power.
>
> Then it happens, every time. Those young people arrive. The Spirit is there. You feel energy, power, clarity of thought. And then they are off to the profound temptations awaiting them at the high school, and you are just Cathy again.
>
> Often, as I look into their faces, I feel overwhelmingly their great, valiant spirits. What a privilege it is to be an instrument in the Lord's hands briefly in their lives! You know, you could set aside study time each day and read and ponder the scriptures, but I'm not sure it would be the same. It is the intensity of trying to impart to them what they need to hear. It's knowing you can't possibly do it without the Lord's help. And then

it's teaching what you've studied and testifying to its truthfulness and correctness and also the huge, stretching sacrifice it seems to be.

Elder Bruce R. McConkie stated, "There is no price too high, no labor too onerous, no struggle too severe, no sacrifice too great, if out of it all we receive and enjoy the gift of the Holy Ghost" (*A New Witness for the Articles of Faith* [Salt Lake City: Deseret Book, 1985], p. 253). I testify that when we keep our spiritual batteries charged, we will hear the voice of the Spirit in our minds and in our hearts. Though it comes as a quiet whispering, a prompting, an impression, it will be heard above the road noise of the world. I testify that the Spirit will work us over, refine us, purify us, cleanse us, and help us in the process of becoming sanctified and redeemed. We should expect to be comforted, chastened, warned, shown our weaknesses, and brought closer to the Savior than we have ever known before.

LEST WE FORGET
TO BELIEVE

A few years ago, after a rather extensive trip to the British Isles during which I had the opportunity to speak to hundreds of young women gathered in many different meetinghouses, I received in the mail a letter that began, "Do you remember me? I was the one in the green jumper on the second row." On another occasion, following a large gathering of young women at a girls' camp in the Northwest, again I received a letter. This young woman did not even question whether I would remember her. She wrote, "After the meeting I stood in line. You hugged me and said something wonderful to me but I can't remember what it was. Would you please write and tell me so that I can put it in my journal and read it when I feel bad?" Of course, I didn't remember exactly what I had told her, but I answered her letter with the message that I usually try to whisper in each young woman's ear as we hug: "Remember, you are a daughter of a Heavenly Father who

loves you. Remember always to stand as a witness of God at all times and in all things and in all places."

Is there anyone who does not have a need, bone-marrow deep, to be remembered? Have you not experienced that feeling?

President Gordon B. Hinckley has said: "I wish I had some way to thank you individually. I hope in the growth of the Church we never forget it is the individual that counts." Once, in a surprise visit to a stake conference in Magna, Utah, he told the Saints, "I did not come here to preach; I just came to tell you I love you." Clearly our prophet recognizes our need to be remembered.

Joseph Smith said, "Nothing is so much calculated to lead people to forsake sin as to take them by the hand, and watch over them with tenderness. When persons manifest the least kindness and love to me, O what power it has over my mind" (*Teachings of the Prophet Joseph Smith,* comp. Joseph Fielding Smith [Salt Lake City: Deseret Book, 1976], p. 240).

One day I happened across a letter in my file that my husband had written many years before. It was a marvelous letter, reminding me in detail of all the wonderful things a wife would like to hear or, more important, to have written to her by her husband. I looked at the date and laid the letter on Heber's desk with a little note, "Is it time for another letter?" In other words, "Do you still remember me?" Later that day, amid the multitude of emergencies demanding attention, he took time to respond. The same letter was returned to my desk with a brief message penciled in on the upper corner. The current date was recorded, along with the word "Reconfirmed" and a smiley face.

We all yearn for the reassurance of being remembered. Even one of the malefactors who hung on the cross said to Jesus,

"Lord, remember me when thou comest into thy kingdom. And Jesus said unto him, Verily I say unto thee, To day shalt thou be with me in paradise" (Luke 23:42–43).

He remembers us. He knows us, knows our names, our thoughts, our hopes, our fears. "Now, this is the truth," wrote George Q. Cannon. "We humble people, we who feel ourselves sometimes so worthless, so good-for-nothing, we are not so worthless as we think. There is not one of us but what God's love has been expended upon. There is not one of us that He has not cared for and caressed" (*Gospel Truth,* 2 vols. [Salt Lake City: Deseret Book, 1974], 1:2).

There may be days when, like my young friend, we may want to ask, "Do you remember me? You hugged me and said something wonderful to me, but I forgot. Can you write and tell me so I can read it when I feel bad?" We might add, "Because I want to be happy." The "great plan of happiness" of which Alma speaks (see Alma 42:8) calls for a "forgetting." Lest we forget, the grand plan is designed entirely to help us return to our Father in Heaven, but an essential part of that plan is the exercise of faith in the Lord Jesus Christ. There is much to be learned from struggle, pain, and sorrow. However, the plan assures eternal happiness, a happiness far greater than we can imagine in mortality. Whatever pains or sorrows or dislocations we may endure, the ultimate definition of happiness must be that we know we have been faithful and that our salvation is assured.

One of the most comforting and reassuring thoughts for me through the years has been, "I chose to come here; I sided with Christ's plan rather than Satan's in the premortal existence." We knew before we were born that we would experience joys and sorrows on this earth, and we eagerly accepted the plan. My

father made this point very clear to me some years ago. I was wrestling with major issues in my life, with prayers not yet answered, or so I thought, and in my mind I heard his words: "My dear, don't trouble yourself about the little things and the big things you agreed to before you came. Remember that you chose this life with its struggles. You chose to accept the forgetting and to see whether you would walk by faith."

It is absolutely essential to our progress that we remember this truth: We made this choice before we arrived here. Wonderfully reassuring scriptures give evidence of many who accepted the blotting out of premortal memory, exercised their faith, kept the commandments, and were assured of their salvation. The road to that eternal salvation requires that we be tried and tested along the way (see D&C 136:31).

So there must be a forgetting. Consider the tender account of little four-year-old Sachi, who kept asking to be left alone with her new baby brother. Finally her parents yielded to her pleadings, but they kept a curious watch outside the baby's bedroom door, which was open a crack. Sachi quietly spoke to the baby, saying, "Baby, tell me what God feels like. I'm starting to forget" (in Jack Canfield and Mark Victor Hansen, *Chicken Soup for the Soul* [Deerfield Beach, Florida: Health Communications, 1993], p. 290).

In her poem "O My Father," Eliza R. Snow expressed her faith in the forgetting that is part of the plan:

> *For a wise and glorious purpose*
> *Thou hast placed me here on earth*
> *And withheld the recollection*
> *Of my former friends and birth.*

But she went on to express something deeper, a feeling of spiritual remembering:

> *Yet ofttimes a secret something*
> *Whispered, "You're a stranger here,"*
> *And I felt that I had wandered*
> *From a more exalted sphere.*
>
> (*Hymns*, no. 292)

Yes, there is a forgetting, but thankfully there's also a remembering, and it is crucial to our inner peace and well-being. To remember is to keep in mind, to retain the thought, to recall, to retrieve, to bring back. This matter of retaining or retrieving is strengthened with keepsakes, mementos, tokens, symbols, CTR rings, journals, and such. Young women have colors as a reminder of the Young Women values. Symbols of this kind stimulate our memories, which then affect our conduct, our attitude, our behavior. As we build and store memories, both good and bad, we are able to progress beyond the events of the past. We gain confidence in making better decisions for the present and the future. Without the gift of memory, we would not be able to see the possibility for growth.

Remember David's response to Saul, who had warned him not to go before Goliath because he was "but a youth." And so he was. However, he had some memorable experiences that he could draw strength from. With confidence, David replied, "The Lord that delivered me out of the paw of the lion, and out of the paw of the bear, he will deliver me out of the hand of this Philistine" (1 Samuel 17:33, 37). How important was it to David and to all of Israel that he remembered how the Lord had blessed

him in the past? How important is it to each of us to remember those times when the Lord made us able to accomplish the mission, the calling, the task given to us?

When we can draw from the past, we don't have to retest every decision or experience. We can turn to our storehouse of memory over and over again and relive precious moments that can sustain, comfort, and protect us against uncertainty and faltering faith.

When Oliver Cowdery began his labors as scribe in the translation of the Book of Mormon, the Lord spoke to him through Joseph Smith as follows: "Behold, thou art Oliver, and I have spoken unto thee because of thy desires; therefore treasure up these words in thy heart. Be faithful and diligent in keeping the commandments of God, and I will encircle thee in the arms of my love." Then he added: "Verily, verily, I say unto you, if you desire a further witness, cast your mind upon the night that you cried unto me in your heart, that you might know concerning the truth of these things. Did I not speak peace to your mind concerning the matter? What greater witness can you have than from God?" (D&C 6:20, 22–23). The Lord seems to be telling him to *remember.* "Remember, Oliver, what I told you before. Treasure those memories, draw strength from them, and never, ever forget." He says to each of us, "Remember those times when I spoke peace to your mind."

Now, if there were an easily dispensed prescription that would provide total and instant recall of what we are learning daily, I would suppose that on the day before final exams there would be a lineup at the pharmacy that would make the line for BYU football tickets appear like a trickle as compared to the mighty Mississippi. When we have spent a great deal of time and effort with our studies, we ought to remember; we want to remember; but oftentimes we don't remember. We know that the information is in our minds somewhere, like on a marvelous computer chip, but the retrieval system is not always dependable. (I've heard of people who claim to have a photographic memory but no same-day delivery. Someone else has said that it is hard to be nostalgic when you can't remember anything.)

This matter of forgetting and remembering seems to play tricks on us as we get older, but I'm not all that worried about our remembering such things as where we put our wallet or the keys to the car or our checkbook or even the information we need to pass our exams. I am more concerned that we remember the experiences that keep us ever mindful of the precious gift of life, its meaning, and all that it offers. We need to remember our covenants, our family relationships, and our homeward journey.

Let's talk about *home* for a moment. Suppose I ran into a former student and said, "Julie, how are you?" And Julie replied, "I feel wonderful today. I just bought my ticket to fly home for Christmas." I would not experience any confusion about where Julie was going or any ambiguity about her sense of joy in knowing she would be with her family. And because I knew that she came from a place halfway around the world, I would also know what the costs were for her travel home, how she had worked and saved and denied herself many luxuries and maybe even some necessities in order to make the trip.

Today Julie could also say in a different sense, "I feel wonderful; I'm on my way home." This life is the time to work and to save and to prepare and, yes, to deny ourselves some things so that we can travel home. The gospel principles help give us a vision of that home. They tell us what to do, how to save, where to buy the ticket, and how much it will cost. A current temple recommend is symbolic of that ticket.

I testify that if we are devotedly intent on returning home, we will be guided in every major decision we have to make throughout our lives—and we will enjoy the journey. Oh, let us remember, lest we forget to believe in that eternal home. I'm convinced that we do not enter this life without strong promptings that there was for each of us a significant before, and there will be a significant after. Because of the biblical account of Christ's death and resurrection, the Christian world at large believes in an afterlife. By comparison, however, very few if any understand that we were born first as spirit children, that we had to make choices before we were born on the earth, and that this mortal life is but one stage in a grand plan. Through revelations given to prophets, we as Latter-day Saints understand more concretely what Dag Hammarskjöld referred to as "coming to conscious recognition of something which we really knew all the time."

President George Q. Cannon gives us this insight: "There is no doubt in my mind that we were familiar with the principles of the Gospel, and though they had faded from our memories, yet when we heard them again the recollection was revived. I believe that when we see our Father in heaven we shall know Him; and the recollection that we were once with Him and that He was our Father will come back to us, and we will fall upon His neck, and He will fall upon us, and we will kiss each other. We will know our Mother, also. We will know those who have begotten us in the spirit world just as much as we will know each other after we pass from this state of existence into another sphere" (*Gospel Truth*, 1:3).

The lessons we were taught in the premortal existence

included the plan for our salvation. The small promptings or inklings of memory we carry into this life are like a lighthouse in the harbor that beckons us home through stormy seas. Faith in the eternal plan helps fill the cavity of emptiness when we feel alone or homesick.

To the young woman who asked the question, "Do you remember me?" I might have responded with another question: "Do *you* remember you? Do you remember who you are and whose you are? Do you remember Him who bought you with a price?"

While we live in this sphere away from home, our Father has equipped us with a remarkable capacity to experience the beauty and abundance of life. Alma exhorts us, "Awake and arouse your faculties" (Alma 32:27). This requires some work and attention on our part. We may look but not see with an eye of faith. We may listen but not hear the whisperings of the Spirit. We may live but without sensitivity.

Do we see and hear and feel the hand of God all around us daily? Korihor seemed to be suffering some form of amnesia when he said to Alma, "Show me a sign, that I may be convinced that there is a God." As Alma pointed out to him: "All things denote there is a God; yea, even the earth, and all things that are upon the face of it, yea, and its motion, yea, and also all the planets which move in their regular form do witness that there is a Supreme Creator" (Alma 30:43–44). After Korihor received his sign and was struck dumb, he put forth his hand and wrote, "I always knew that there was a God" (Alma 30:52). He remembered too late.

When we follow the direction of the great plan of happiness, we receive confirmation upon confirmation that the Lord's

mission was and is exactly what he claimed it to be: "To bring to pass the immortality and eternal life of man" (Moses 1:39). It is our mortal memory of these confirmations that allows us to have faith in Christ.

At the close of his mortal ministry, knowing what was ahead, Jesus prepared the apostles for the challenges he knew would come. As they were assembled in that upper room, he promised: "The Comforter, which is the Holy Ghost, whom the Father will send in my name, he shall teach you all things, and bring all things to your remembrance, whatsoever I have said unto you. Peace I leave with you, my peace I give unto you: not as the world giveth, give I unto you. Let not your heart be troubled, neither let it be afraid" (John 14:26–27).

Then he provided them with a sacred ordinance that would help them remember his promises. He "took bread and blessed it, and brake, and gave to them, and said, Take it, and eat. Behold, this is for you to do in remembrance of my body; for as oft as ye do this ye will remember this hour that I was with you. And he took the cup, and when he had given thanks, he gave it to them; and they all drank of it. And he said unto them . . . as oft as ye do this ordinance, ye will remember me in this hour that I was with you and drank with you of this cup, even the last time in my ministry" (JST, Mark 14:20–24).

Will we ever be absent from those occasions each week when we are invited, even as the apostles, to eat and drink and remember the Savior, the Son of God? Does not this remembering make us better able to keep his commandments, so that we can always have his Spirit to be with us? Think how we would feel if these sacred emblems were not available to us because of our lack of worthiness to partake of them. Would we be more ready, more reverent, more thoughtful and grateful when the opportunity was restored?

I know someone in that situation. He tells me that each week he hears the words of the sacrament prayers with a clarity, a fervor, a commitment that he never felt before. But as the emblems of the bread and the water are offered him, he must pass them on to others who often seem not to feel the full impact of what they are doing. His heart cries out, "Do you realize the blessing that is yours?"

Another ordinance that helps in our spiritual remembering is that of baptism. With the gift of the Holy Ghost bestowed after our baptism, we are entitled to a special kind of direction and guidance that will create sustaining memories. The covenant of baptism—and the renewal of that covenant through the ordinance of the sacrament—admits us to a very select environment in this mortal world. Whatever our loneliness and isolation, we can know that our Heavenly Father knows us personally and loves us, and his spirit can and will always attend us.

I'm deeply impressed by the last years of Moroni's life. He was alone. All of his friends and family had been killed. He had to hide himself from his enemies. He was always on the move, trying to find his own shelter and to sustain himself physically, all the while keeping secure the sacred records his father had entrusted to him. He was a mortal like you and me, but during all those long years of trial and loneliness, he was sustained by what we hear each week in the sacramental prayer. He always remembered Christ, he kept His commandments, and he had His Spirit to be with him.

Finally Moroni was able to express his remarkable testimony, to figuratively look each of us in the eye and say, "I exhort you to remember" (Moroni 10:27). My urgent plea is that we remember, lest we forget to believe. We may not remember all of the equations, the formulas, the histories, the prescriptions that become a part of our formal education, but let us remember and never forget:

> *God loved us, so he sent his Son,*
> *Christ Jesus, the atoning One,*
> *To show us by the path he trod*
> *The one and only way to God.*
>
> (*Hymns*, no. 187)

YOUR OWN PIECE
OF MARBLE

*T*he story is told of a great sculptor who worked on a large piece of marble day after day, week after week, patiently and persistently cutting, carving, and carefully creating a masterpiece. During this time a young child had been observing the ongoing efforts of this great sculptor. One day she announced with excitement as she viewed his work: "I know who that is! That's Abraham Lincoln." Curious, she asked the sculptor, "How did you know he was in there?"

As children of our Heavenly Father, we need to develop faith in his knowledge that "we're in there." When we have an understanding of who we are—of our divine heritage and our great potential—we will realize that all the painful chipping away is to rid us of all that isn't us, to free us to become who we really are. Within each of us lies the workmanship of the Master, and we can reach our full potential only if we have the sustained commitment to subject ourselves to the sharp, cutting edge of the sculptor's knife. Our vision is limited, but He knows who we are and who we are to become.

I am reminded of a fellow who asked his wife one early morning, "Well, dear, how did you find yourself this morning?" She responded, "Silly, I just threw back the covers and there I was." The sobering reality is that some people haven't found themselves, whether it is under the covers, inside the block of marble, or anywhere. They don't even know where to look.

When I was a child growing up in a rural area, one of our favorite games was hide-and-seek. I liked that game until the time I hid under a pile of straw in the barn and nobody found me. I waited and waited and didn't get found. When I came out, the kids were gone, except my older brother, who was anxious to tease me. "Dummy," he said. "You're supposed to get found." I have discovered since then that my brother was right. We need to get found, not only by others, but more importantly by ourselves.

My point could be summarized with these words: Get found. Don't hide under a bushel or a haystack. Carve away everything that isn't you. Don't hide from others or from yourself. Find yourself, not just under the covers or the hay. You are in the wonderful process of creation, breaking free from your block of marble.

Some years ago, while helping develop instructional television programs for the elementary schools in Utah, I learned a great lesson about the blessing of struggle. The idea was to provide a field-trip experience through television that would not otherwise be available to the students. I remember well the filming at a chicken hatchery just outside of Logan. On the first visit we filmed the carefully selected eggs being placed in large incubator trays. As each tray was filled, it was pushed into a heat-controlled unit. That was about all there was to see on the first visit.

Twenty-one days later, we returned. Things were quite different this time. There was a lot to observe. When a tray was pulled out, we witnessed a miracle: such energy, exertion, activity, and force, we could hardly believe it. The little chickens were breaking free from the shells that held them captive. But I learned that not all good chickens hatch at the same time. While some were completely out of their shells, others were still in the process of pecking away. I held one egg in my hand that had not yet had a break in the shell. Though there were no obvious signs of progress, I could feel through the shell a pulsation that was steady and strong. Growth was taking place, even if it was not yet visible to the eye. That miracle of life held captive was struggling to get free.

I had an idea. I picked up one egg that had only a tiny crack in the shell and, with the camera focused on the egg, I proceeded to very carefully break away the shell, bit by bit, thus assisting the little chicken in the hatching. The cameraman got some good shots, and I was pleased that the children would be able to witness this miracle of hatching on film.

That is, I was pleased until the manager of the hatchery explained to me that I had not assisted the little chicken by helping it hatch. What I had actually done was to remove the struggle that was required for it to develop the capacity to survive outside its shell. He informed me that the little chicken I had released from its shell and its struggle would surely die.

Since that memorable experience, I have witnessed over and over again the growth, the strength, the power, the capacity that

gradually evolves while the struggle for hatching takes place— not in chickens, but in people. Young or old, we are all in the process of hatching, breaking out of our shells, freeing ourselves and releasing the masterpiece, the miracle, held within. It isn't easy, and it isn't intended to be. The struggle is designed to strengthen us and prepare us for opportunities far greater than we can now realize. It is through our tests that we find ourselves by releasing ourselves from the influences of the world that would otherwise hold us captive.

An old hymn proclaims, "Let each man learn to know himself; To gain that knowledge let him labor"(*Hymns,* 1948, no. 91). Whether consciously or not, beginning at a tender age, we all yearn for an answer to the question, Who am I?

Oh, that we might have the opportunity to explain to everyone about our true identity and what it means to become sons and daughters of Jesus Christ! A young elder in our mission, bold yet gentle, one day in the park approached an elderly gentleman. He opened his mouth to bear testimony to this stranger concerning what he knew to be true. The older man, touched by the Spirit, asked the young missionary, "Who are you, anyway?" The missionary responded with conviction, "I am an ambassador of the Lord Jesus Christ, and I have come with a message for you." When we come to know who we are, we too will be better prepared to speak out and stand as witnesses of God at all times.

In the eternal and spiritual dimension, a more significant question comes into play: *Whose* am I? How I wish every man and woman, young and old, had a conviction of the truth taught in the Young Women values: "I am a child of a Heavenly Father who loves me, and I will have faith in his eternal plan, which centers in Jesus Christ, my Savior."

If our identity is determined by the standards of the world, our sense of self-worth will always be conditional upon our position, our possessions, our performance, our appearance, our being accepted socially. People who don't know who they are or whose they are tend to wander from the straight and narrow path searching to find themselves. Many groups offer membership and acceptance—if we will relinquish citizenship in God's kingdom. But those who wear those groups' symbols and follow their identifying behaviors will soon find that they have been betrayed and that they are lost, not found. From my association with people young and older, I have become convinced that questionable and sometimes totally unacceptable behavior stems from a loss of identity. Without a sense of our true identity, we can be lost to society.

I am impressed by the statement, "You did not come to this world to get your worth; you brought it with you." I know of nothing that I value more than the assurance that we have an eternal Father in Heaven; a Savior of mankind, who is Jesus Christ; and a Holy Spirit who can testify to us of our identity, our covenant relationship. We have already chosen our team, our captain, our goal. There is no dual citizenship in this plan. One cannot live in Zion, as someone has said, and maintain a summer home in Babylon. As Latter-day Saints, our identity is apart from all the rest of the world. Our direction is different and our purpose is different.

When we went into the waters of baptism, we entered into a covenant relationship with Jesus Christ "to be obedient to his commandments in all things that he shall command us, all the remainder of our days" (Mosiah 5:5). Through that covenant relationship, we became his sons and his daughters. "For behold, this day he hath spiritually begotten you; for ye say that your hearts are changed through faith on his name; therefore, ye are born of him and have become his sons and his daughters" (Mosiah 5:7).

If you should have days when you feel worthless, good for nothing, reread that passage of scripture; it will clarify your identity, your direction, your purpose, and your relationship with our Father in Heaven. See beyond the clouds. Pass the barriers and walk by faith.

Yes, the struggle is real. It must be, if we are to break from the spiritual shell and become all God intends us to be. But we are not left alone to find the way. We know the path, and others before us have succeeded. Because of God's great love for us, he has provided the way for our victory, if we will just do our part.

Consider the change in Alma the Younger's life when he was visited by an angel and given an understanding of who he was. Saul, on the road to Damascus, changed from a persecutor of the church to a powerful missionary, Paul, who became an apostle of the Lord. When Jesus stretched forth his hand and caught Peter as he began to sink in the water, saying, "O thou of little faith, wherefore didst thou doubt?" (Matthew 14:31), the Lord knew that Peter was not yet the man he would become. "When thou art converted, strengthen thy brethren," he admonished his chief disciple at the Last Supper (Luke 22:32). Even Peter had some growing yet to do.

Of course, there are times when it is hard, very hard. It is hard to take a stand and defend what is right when it isn't popular or enjoyable and no one seems to appreciate our values. We may be worrying about finances or health, grades or friends. Relationships are difficult and family problems are real and often it seems that no one understands. Sometimes selfishness and pride get a strong hold, honesty is not popular, and immorality is flaunted on every side. Self-discipline is a lifetime process, and a crucial one. It has been said that where there is no discipline, Christ has no disciple.

The Book of Mormon prophet Enos gave us a pattern that we might follow. "My soul hungered," he wrote, "and I kneeled down before my Maker, and I cried unto him in mighty prayer and supplication for mine own soul" (Enos 1:4). He heard the voice of the Lord in his mind and heart, saying that his sins were forgiven because of his faith in Christ. Once he had found himself and was at peace with himself and with the Lord, his first concern was for the welfare of his brethren. He began to pray and labor with all diligence in their behalf.

This is a pattern that has been repeated over and over, both then and now, by true disciples. When we find ourselves, we feel an immediate concern for the welfare and happiness of others. The Lord has indicated this as a way to identify true disciples: "A new commandment I give unto you, That ye love one another; as I have loved you, that ye also love one another. By this shall all men know that ye are my disciples, if ye have love one to another" (John 13:34–35).

For each of us there will be times in the privacy of our own souls when we must be prepared to answer the question, Who are you? And from the depths of our understanding, with the truth borne of the Spirit, we can join our voices with a chorus of thousands: I am a disciple of the Lord Jesus Christ.

A TIME FOR CLEANSING

Every Monday morning like clockwork, on time and on schedule, the garbage truck comes down our street, stopping at each home along the way. Each week we have waiting for it at least one large black container, looking on the outside like everyone else's garbage container up and down the street. However, if the contents of all those containers were to be exposed and examined, they would likely vary in some interesting ways.

In our kitchen we have a garbage disposal. To rid ourselves of the unwanted material we flip a switch and then turn on the water, which washes away the garbage and leaves the sink clean, free from any debris. Thank goodness we have these reliable systems for clearing the garbage from our lives!

But let's think for a moment about mental or spiritual "garbage." Many people struggle with feelings of inadequacy, unworthiness, lack of knowledge, and even weakness of testimony and faith (or so they think, often because their faith has not yet been fully tested). Some have made wrong choices and are harrowed up in their souls; the burdens become heavier each day. If such garbage is not emptied, the results can be devastating.

President Spencer W. Kimball taught, "In the armory of thought, weapons are formed by which men destroy themselves." We must cleanse our lives of these destructive weapons if we are to progress. For some, the cleansing must begin by getting rid of thoughts of self-deprecation. We can't stop thinking, of course— but we can change our thoughts.

I remember being taught as a child in Sunday School class that we shouldn't think bad words. I tried hard not to think bad words. I didn't want to think bad words; I wanted to be good. One day I made up my mind to never think a bad word. In my heart I thought of the two worst words that I knew and promised to never say them or think them again. The harder I tried not to think of them, the more those words seemed to play across the screen of my mind. I was plagued by my sins and felt helpless in stopping these thoughts, which jumped into my mind even as I knelt to pray.

We used to have what we called a Sunday School "memory gem." Every Sunday morning we would recite a few lines that we were supposed to then carry in our thoughts all week long. One of those gems, which I still remember from my childhood, proved to be the answer to my dilemma:

> *Purify our hearts, our Savior.*
> *Let us go not far astray,*
> *That we may be counted worthy*
> *Of thy Spirit day by day.*

I could not stop thinking negative things, but with the Savior's help I could replace my unfruitful thoughts with positive ones. That discovery became a powerful source of strength in subsequent years, and I continue to repeat that simple but profound little gem in those moments when other thoughts would crowd in if there were a crack left open. As we carry the burdens that are part of this probationary period, there are many things that we cannot control, but our thoughts we can.

On occasion when I would speak with a missionary whose thoughts seemed to be weighing him down, I would ask, "Ere you left your room this morning, did you think to pray? When your heart was filled with anger, did you think to pray?" (see *Hymns*, no. 140). And then I would ask another question that seemed always to catch their attention: "When you prayed, did you *think?*"

Our thoughts, our words, our deeds make us what we are. King Benjamin, after his important address to the people gathered at the temple, summarized his concerns for them: "If ye do not watch yourselves, and your thoughts, and your words, and your deeds, and observe the commandments of God, and continue in the faith of what ye have heard concerning the coming of our Lord, even unto the end of your lives, ye must perish. And now, O man, remember, and perish not" (Mosiah 4:30).

I believe that to perish is to have the Spirit withdrawn, to bear the burden of darkness and despair. If our whole bodies are to be filled with light (see D&C 88:67), we must "cast away [our] idle thoughts" (D&C 88:69). The Lord counsels, "Look unto me in every thought; doubt not, fear not" (D&C 6:36). Our doubts and our fears can imprison us and hold us hostage. We must exchange them for messages that free us—messages of faith, not fear.

In Proverbs 23:7 we read, "As [a man] thinketh in his heart, so is he." President David O. McKay said this on the subject: "No principle of life was more constantly emphasized by the Great Teacher than the necessity of right thinking. To Him, the man was not what he appeared to be outwardly, nor what he professed to be by his words: what the man *thought* determined in all cases what the man *was*. No teacher emphasized more strongly than He the truth that 'as a man thinketh in his heart, so is he.' With him the deadly sins were not neglect of the ritual, nor even crimes punishable by the laws of all civilized nations, but wrong ideas, motives and feelings" (*Instructor,* September 1958, p. 257).

When we can control our thoughts, eliminate criticism, feelings of pride, negativism, doubt, and fear, then we, like the people in King Benjamin's day, will have a mighty change in our hearts, "that we have no more disposition to do evil, but to do good continually" (Mosiah 5:2). From an article titled "The Doctrine of Christ" by Larry E. Dahl we read:

> If conversion can be considered a gradual process wherein we overcome one sin today and another tomorrow, at what point does the Holy Ghost come to convey the remission of sins and change our heart? Perhaps the answer to this question is that the Holy Ghost comes quietly each time we overcome a particular sin or weakness, bringing peace of conscience concerning that part of our life, and strengthening our desire to do right. Continuing this process qualifies us eventually for a remission of all of our sins—a complete baptism of fire. To be complete, the baptism of fire and of the Holy Ghost, like the baptism of water, requires full immersion. . . .
>
> Before being born of the Spirit, a person hungers and thirsts after the things of the world, while dutifully performing the things of God; *after* the baptism of fire, a person

hungers and thirsts after the things of the Spirit, while duti-
fully performing necessary worldly things. (In Monte S.
Nyman and Charles D. Tate, eds., *The Book of Mormon: Second
Nephi, The Doctrinal Structure* [Provo, Utah: Religious Studies
Center, Brigham Young University, 1989], pp. 365, 367)

The process of cleansing the vessel by eradicating inappropriate thoughts should not really be likened to pushing the but-
ton on the garbage disposal and having the mess taken neatly
away. It requires continuous, arduous, daily effort to control our
thoughts. Satan fights with psychological warfare. We cannot
allow him to use his insidious weapons, from the extreme of
pornography to the habit of criticism to inappropriate TV programs, videos, music, and on and on. Our minds become the
battleground. Pure thoughts are the weapons that conquer the
enemy. It is not a task to be trivialized.

However, just as the accumulation of physical garbage is carried away from our homes each week, there is a weekly process
provided to assist in our spiritual cleansing. As we partake of the
sacrament, we have a glorious opportunity to reflect and repent
and renew our determination to remember and follow Christ.

We are responsible for our thoughts. Our thoughts, our
words, our deeds make us what we are. Let us be diligent each
week in keeping our schedule with the cleansing mechanism that
prevents us from an accumulation of unwanted garbage. May we
understand the privilege accorded us by the Savior that allows us
to cleanse the vessel and lay down the burden.

A LEGACY OF FAITH THROUGH THE BOOK OF MORMON

*I*n the last recorded words of Moroni, ancient prophet and modern messenger, he testifies of the truthfulness of the Book of Mormon, with a promise to all who will ask with a sincere heart, with real intent, and having faith in Christ, that by the power of the Holy Ghost they too may know the truth of all things (see Moroni 10:4–5). As surely as this pattern is followed, the promised blessing of testimony of the Book of Mormon will come.

The first member of every family to gain a testimony of the Book of Mormon and stay true to that testimony begins a legacy of faith for generations yet to come. For many the legacy began generations ago. For others, recent converts, they begin the legacy with their own testimony. When personal testimonies of the Book of Mormon are recorded and accumulated from one generation to the next, these precious accounts contribute in a significant way to passing on the legacy of faith bonded by testimonies of the Book of Mormon.

Edwin Kent Greene and Julia Leavitt Greene, with modest accumulations of this world's wealth, left to their children a document concerning the disbursement of their valuable possessions. The document begins: "The last will and testament of Edwin Kent Greene and Julia Leavitt Greene to their family, their companions, and family as are or may be, We leave with you our testimony that God lives, that Jesus Christ, the Only Begotten in the flesh, also lives and has restored the everlasting gospel in our day to his prophet, Joseph Smith, by revelation and heavenly messengers as needed for the salvation of mankind." They continue their testimony and close with these words, "May your hearts ever be open and your feelings tender towards these great truths, is our humble prayer." They departed this life leaving to their posterity their most valuable possession: their testimony of the gospel of Jesus Christ as contained in the Book of Mormon.

How priceless this bit of history is to those in our family line! However, the story has a much earlier beginning. Edwin Kent Greene's mother, Adelene Allen, was born in Syderstone, Norfolk, England, on April 19, 1865. One evening when she was twenty-one years of age, Annie, as she was called, and her dear friend Patty Bennett were out shopping when they heard two men singing, "Come, listen to a prophet's voice and hear the word of God." They drew near and stood spellbound through a Mormon street meeting. They read the Book of Mormon and received fervent testimonies of its truthfulness. Annie's family was bitterly opposed to her joining the Mormon church. For the first time in her life she found herself forced to disobey her parents. Fearful of being persuaded to remain in England, she did not tell her family of her conversion to the Church or her plans to emigrate until after she left for America. The first letter she received from her mother revealed tender feelings: "My dearest daughter. Whatever on earth has caused you to go out of your own country and away from all your friends I cannot imagine. You say, 'don't fret.' How do you think I can help it when such a blow as that comes to strike me all out in a heap? You say you are happy, but I can't think it, for I am sure I could not have been happy to have gone into a foreign country and left you behind. You say you will come again, but I don't think you'll hesitate your life over the deep waters again. When I think about it I feel wretched. You had a good place and a good home to come to whenever you like. And I must say that I love the very ground you walked upon. And now I am left to fret in this world, but still all the same for that, I wish you good luck and hope the Lord will prosper you in every way. I remain your loving mother."

Adelene Allen married Daniel Kent Greene, whose mother was Susan Kent. In the life sketch of Susan Kent Greene written by her daughter Lula Greene Richards we read:

> Susan was nearly sixteen years old when tidings of the religious works of the Prophet Joseph Smith were brought to the notice of her near kindred and herself who were staunch Methodists. Her father, Daniel Kent, like other real Methodists, believed in prayer, and morning and evening called his family together and they all knelt and unitedly gave thanks for all blessings bestowed by our Heavenly Father and asked for continued help and guidance. And after careful reading and studying of the Book of Mormon, the following beautiful testimony of its truth was given to that honest worshiper and his devoted family. One morning while they were

engaged in family prayer, the head of the household, as usual, voicing the united petitions, his speech was suddenly changed to another language new and not understood by any of the family but the speaker himself. This remarkable and unexpected manifestation of an unseen power before the petition was ended simply changed again to the supplicant's usual manner of speech, giving a clear interpretation of the words which had been spoken in the unknown language. That interpretation was a strong and powerful declaration of the truth of the Book of Mormon and the divinity of the calling and work of the Prophet Joseph Smith.

Susan's conviction of the truth of the gospel restored to the earth in the latter days was so strong that she could not reject it, although to join the hated and reviled Church of Jesus Christ of Latter-day Saints cost her so great a sacrifice that it came near taking her life. For two days and nights friends and family of which she was a favorite member all mourned her as dead. The sacrifice she had to make was the giving up of the affections of a young man to whom she had given her maiden love with very high hopes of future happiness, but whose worldly pride would not allow him to have anything to do with one who favored the new religion of which he heard so much evil spoken. When Susan became convinced of this fact concerning her lover, so deep was the wound occasioned to her sensitive heart that she could partake of no nourishment, and after some days she relapsed into a coma so profound that it had the appearance of actual death and was so considered and mourned over by those about her. But at 5 P.M. in the afternoon of the second day of her deathlike sleep, as the clock was striking, Susan's eyes opened and she said to her mother, who was bending over her, "five o'clock, how long have I slept."

Lula Greene Richards also wrote concerning the testimony of her grandmother, my great-great-grandmother Rhoda Young Greene (Brigham Young's sister):

> When Rhoda was twenty-four years old she was married to John P. Greene. He was a Methodist circuit preacher. All the Youngs and their close associates were Methodists at that time. Their first introduction to the Mormons or Mormonism was through a Book of Mormon being left with Rhoda by Samuel H. Smith, the Prophet Joseph Smith's brother. Mrs. Greene requested her husband to read the book, telling him the manner recommended by the missionary of how he could receive a testimony. He read the sacred volume. He prayed about what he read. He was convinced of the truth found within its pages. Within a short time he and Mrs. Greene were ready for baptism. The Greenes loaned this copy of the Book of Mormon to Phineas Young, Mrs. Greene's brother. It was next handed to his brother, Brigham Young, and from him to Mrs. Murray, his sister and the mother of Heber C. Kimball's wife. She believed it. Heber and his wife read it. They "received the work without hesitancy." Mother Smith, commenting on this, said: "Thus was this book the means of convincing his whole family and bringing them into the Church, where they have continued faithful members from the commencement of their career until now. And through their faithfulness and zeal, some of them have become as great and honorable men as ever stood upon the earth."

At the time of his wife's passing, John P. Greene prepared her obituary as follows:

> Dear Sir. I wish you to insert in the *Times and Seasons* the obituary of the wife of my youth, Rhoda Young Greene, sister

of Brigham Young. She departed this life being 51 years, four months, and eight days old. In the month of May, 1829, she received the Book of Mormon and on the first reading believed it a true history and longed to see the author and the despised people. And in the month of April 1831 we first heard the gospel preached. When she heard she believed with all her heart and immediately obeyed the heavenly mandate. And on the morning of the 13th of April, we were baptized for the remission of our sins and from that hour, her heart was fixed on gathering, living, and suffering with the saints of the last days. A watchful follower of Christ, inflexible in every duty, and finally was perfected in suffering and died a martyr to the religion of our Lord Jesus Christ and I believe will have a part in the first resurrection. Believe me dear brother, your affectionate friend and brother in the Lord, John P. Greene. (*Times and Seasons,* February 15, 1841, p. 325)

Testimonies of the Book of Mormon are also carried through the family line of Julia Leavitt Greene. From the history of her great-great-grandmother, Sarah Studevant Leavitt, we read: "Raised in New Hampshire by Presbyterian parents, young Sarah Studevant regularly studied the Bible and prayed on her own. . . . [She] married Jeremiah Leavitt in 1817, and the young couple moved to Hatley, Quebec, Canada. . . . There were Mormon elders in Canada in the 1830s, but none of them found their way to Hatley. A traveler who had attended a Mormon gathering elsewhere loaned the Leavitts a copy of the Book of Mormon and Parley P. Pratt's *A Voice of Warning.* 'We believed them without preaching,' Jeremiah Leavitt later wrote." (Kenneth W. Godfrey, Audrey M. Godfrey, and Jill Mulvay Derr, *Women's Voices: An Untold History of the Latter-day Saints, 1830–1900* [Salt Lake City: Deseret Book, 1982], p. 26).

We read from Sarah's journal:

I had a place that I went every day for secret prayers. My mind would be carried away in prayer so that I knew nothing of what was going on around me. It seemed like a cloud was resting down over my head. If that cloud would break, there was an angel that had a message for me or some new light. If the cloud would break, there would be something new and strange revealed. I did not know that it concerned anyone but myself. Soon after this there was one of my husband's sisters came in, and after spending a short time in the house she asked me to take a walk with her. She had heard the gospel preached by a Mormon and believed it and been baptized. She commenced and related the whole of Joseph's vision and what the Angel Moroni had said, the mission he had called him to.

It came to my mind in a moment that this was the message that was behind that cloud, for me and not for me only, but for the whole world, and I considered it of more importance than anything I had ever heard before. . . .

I read the Book of Mormon, the Doctrine and Covenants, and all the writings I could get from the Latter-day Saints. . . . I sought with my whole heart a knowledge of the truth and obtained a knowledge that never has nor never will leave me. (Godfrey, Godfrey, and Derr, *Women's Voices,* pp. 30–31)

As we read and study the Book of Mormon, the spirit of the book penetrates into our hearts, and we come to really know and love our Lord and Savior Jesus Christ. We become more aware of his infinite love for us. We learn of the Atonement and of the way to salvation provided through the ordinances and covenants of the gospel of Jesus Christ. We learn how to qualify ourselves for all the blessings our Father has in store for his children who are obedient. We learn how to repent and how to forgive and how to love one another as our Savior loves us. We gain a long-ing, an intense desire to be with him and be like him.

While some have a long history of connection with the Book of Mormon, others have only a beginning. In the mission field, we encouraged each missionary to write a brief commentary of each chapter of the Book of Mormon concerning what the mes-sage meant to him or her personally. At the conclusion, they were asked to write their own testimonies to future generations, even as Moroni had done.

One young elder, the first in his family line to have a testi-mony of the Book of Mormon, wrote in his commentary: "This record I have made is true, for I made it with mine own hands. In making this commentary I have gained a powerful knowledge that the Book of Mormon is the word of God. No man without divine help could have written this book. Also I know of its truthfulness because of the Holy Ghost. He has shown me in my heart and mind that it is true. I need not stand before Moroni to find out that Jesus Christ is my Savior. I know that the book is from God." He further testified of the Prophet Joseph Smith and all aspects of the book, and then concluded: "Lastly, from writ-ing this commentary I have come to know Jesus Christ. He lives. His voice speaks to the soul as we read the Book of Mormon. It contains his word. Therefore we have a clear guide as to how we are to act before him. Jesus Christ loved us very much. He left nothing undone for our salvation. This Church is true. We are His. He purchased our souls with his perfect blood. He is our master, yet we are free. In his name I finish this record. In the name of Jesus Christ. Amen."

Who is to say what the worth of that testimony will be to his posterity in twenty, forty, or a hundred years from now? It has been my experience when skimming through journals, past and present, that those entries relative to the Book of Mormon become beacons of light from one generation to the next. Wherever we stand, with lengthy or brief family histories related to the Book of Mormon, these records become a powerful and precious legacy of faith.

THE DEEPER THE COMMITMENT, THE RICHER THE BLESSINGS

The story is told of a young girl learning to roller-skate. It seems she took a terrible fall, skinned her knee severely, and of course began to cry loudly enough to bring her mother running to her rescue. But before her mother had an opportunity to comfort her or console her, the little girl had stopped crying, much to her mother's surprise. She asked, "Why did you stop so quickly, my dear?" The little girl responded with conviction, "Because I told myself to, and then I made myself mind me." When we are committed to "make ourselves mind us," to make the demands of the flesh submissive to the spirit, we have won a great victory that will open doors to opportunity, freedom, and abundant blessings.

Hanging on the wall just at the foot of the bed where I slept as a child was a rather rough, unfinished piece of wood bearing the printed message: "Happiness lies not in doing the things you like to do, but in learning to like the things you have to do." That never made much sense to me during those early years, but I have since discovered the wisdom and the prophetic truth in that simple statement. When we are committed to the things we "have to do," we prepare ourselves to receive all the blessings our Father has promised.

A commitment is a pledge, a vow, a determination, a promise, a resolution. Our understanding of and commitment to the covenants we have made with God are essential to our well-being now and in the eternities. Elder Theodore M. Burton warned: "The closer we approach the second coming of Jesus Christ, the greater will be Satan's efforts. . . . Unless we live very close to God and listen carefully to the whisperings of the Holy Spirit, we will find dissension creeping into our own lives" (in Conference Report, October 1974, p. 77). We should expect life to be difficult, because we are to be tried and tested in all things. It is in those very trials and tests that we discover and demonstrate the level of our commitment.

Joshua showed his commitment when he said, "Choose you this day whom ye will serve . . . but as for me and my house, we will serve the Lord" (Joshua 24:15). Nephi taught us of commitment when he said, "I will go and do" (1 Nephi 3:7). He didn't say "later" or "maybe" or "sometime." Moroni declared his commitment, "I, Moroni, will not deny the Christ; wherefore, I wander whithersoever I can for the safety of mine own life" (Moroni 1:3). Paul committed himself on the road to Damascus when he asked, "Lord, what wilt thou have me to do?" (Acts 9:6). Mary, the mother of Jesus, spoke these words of commitment: "Be it unto me according to thy word" (Luke 1:38). And Jesus said to his disciples: "If any man will come after me, let him deny himself, and take up his cross, and follow me. For whosoever will save his life shall lose it: and whosoever will lose his life for my sake shall find it" (Matthew 16:24–25). Are these scriptural examples of commitment mere stories? Will we read them as history and then close the book, or do they fire us with a burning desire to consecrate all that we are, all that we have to the Lord?

Among our missionaries we saw a degree of commitment paralleled in few other places, and with that level of commitment we witnessed blessings and physical evidence of miracles happening every day. Total commitment brings a living, driving, encompassing force that comes like a new birth. These young men and young women begin to see new meaning in life, with increased faith and hope and promise. As they come to know the Savior and to realize the price paid in their behalf, their commitment is intensified. Sometimes the days are long. The demands are exacting. The rejection is discouraging. Yet they come and they serve valiantly because of their commitment to themselves, to their families, and to their Father in Heaven. They work day after day, and just one baptism rewards them a hundredfold.

One young elder, after a few months of struggle and resistance to self-discipline and only partial commitment, wrote the following letter one day, "Dear President, This diligence and obedience stuff you've been talking about is really beginning to kick in." After he became committed, he had a mighty change of heart. He began to love everything and everyone. The battle inside subsided and he became a powerful, happy, effective missionary.

The commitments and the blessings are not reserved for those in the mission field. We are all away from home for a season, on a mission, so to speak. We hear the same counsel in meeting after meeting, time after time, lesson after lesson, over and over again. But one day, one time, we listen—and once we get the vision of what the grand plan of happiness is all about, we become converted. Once we have resolved the inner conflict and made up our minds, we have achieved a private victory, and a new, spiritual perspective fills our lives. We understand what President Spencer W. Kimball said, "Since immortality and eternal life constitute the sole purpose of life, all other interests and activities are but incidental thereto."

W. H. Murray wrote, "Until one is committed, there is hesitancy, the chance to draw back, always ineffectiveness. Concerning all acts of initiative and creation, there is one elementary truth, the ignorance of which kills countless ideas and splendid plans: that the moment one definitely commits oneself, then providence moves too. All sorts of things occur to help one that would never otherwise have occurred. A whole stream of events issue from the decision, rising in one's favor, all manner of unforeseen incidences and meetings and material assistance, which no man could have dreamt would have come his way."

I am always inspired by the commitment of our early pioneers, one of whom testified: "I have pulled my handcart when I was so weak and weary from illness and lack of food that I could hardly put one foot ahead of the other. I have looked ahead and seen a patch of sand or a hill slope and I have said, I can only go that far and there I must give up, for I cannot pull the load through it. I have gone on to that sand and when I reached it, the cart began pushing me. I have looked back many times to see who was pushing my cart, but my eyes saw no one. I knew then that the angels of God were there" (as quoted by James E. Faust, *Ensign*, May 1979, p. 53).

We are pioneers on a new frontier. We may not have to push a handcart to the valley, but it may be harder to push away an invitation to a particular movie or a style of clothing or an inappropriate party, to push away the temptation for Sabbath day recreation or the tendency for anger or criticism or pride. When we are determined with every fiber of our being that nothing will stop us from our commitment to follow Christ at all costs, the angels will push our cart and we will make it home.

I think of one of our elders, the only member of the Church in his family, who showed incredible diligence and faith. Two thousand doors in one month—five hundred every week—was his goal. He bore testimony that when his strength was expended near the end of each week, it was as though he was being carried with hardly any effort at all to that last door. He and his faithful companion gained more appointments to teach than ever before.

I think of a dear sister who was told by her father that if she left for a mission there would be no place for her at home when she returned. She came to our mission, but her commitment wavered temporarily and she struggled and wanted to go home. She wondered why she had ever come in the first place. At first she agreed to stay two more days, then just till the end of the week, then one more week. Finally one day she committed herself to stay no matter what, and from that moment on she was a different person. Once she made the commitment, she was free from the gripping fear of discouragement, despondency, and doubt. She became one of our most effective missionaries. Meanwhile, in answer to her fervent prayers, the Lord was blessing her family at home. Her father became actively involved in the Church and accepted a calling as a stake missionary. Upon her return, the family was sealed in the temple.

How important is one person's commitment? How might others be blessed by our own self-discipline? By contrast, how many blessings are lost by those who, refusing to make a commitment, "return again to their own place, to enjoy that which they are willing to receive, because they were not willing to enjoy that which they might have received" (D&C 88:32).

We might gauge our own level of commitment by how we answer these questions posed by President Howard W. Hunter: "Am I a true and living member? . . . Am I deeply and fully dedicated to keeping the covenants I have made with the Lord? Am I totally committed to living the gospel and being a doer of the word and not a hearer only? Do I live my religion? Will I remain true? Do I stand firm against Satan's temptations?" (*That We Might Have Joy* [Salt Lake City: Deseret Book, 1994], p. 149).

Why, we may ask, are we always being pressed for deeper commitment? There are many whys, but the grand why is so that our Father in Heaven can shower us with all the blessings he has for those who love him and keep his commandments. Our Father in Heaven knows us. He asks each of us to commit not a particle more than we can give, but not a particle less. He doesn't want just our money or our time or our work; he wants *us*—all of us, heart and soul, all that we are and all that we might yet become. He wants our total commitment, and in return we are invited to come and partake of the blessings, to become joint heirs with Jesus Christ.

Someone asked the famous musician Ann Softy Muta how she could spend so much time on her music, depriving herself of many other experiences and opportunities. She responded, "What else I couldn't do didn't matter because I had what I wanted." And then the question, "How can you practice so long when there is no one there, no audience to listen?" brought her answer, "If no one is there, I am there to hear it, and I am serving the composer, the one who made the music."

Even when no one seems to be listening or watching or caring, let us be totally committed, steadfast and immovable. The Lord tells us, "Be faithful, keep my commandments, and ye shall inherit the kingdom of heaven" (D&C 6:37). Can we ask for more? May God bless us to claim our inheritance, recognizing that the deeper our commitment is, the richer our blessings will be.

LIVING WATER TO QUENCH
SPIRITUAL THIRST

I wish we were in a situation where we might exchange thoughts and feelings. We would talk and listen and cheer each other on. We would pray for and with each other and laugh and cry, mend and heal, rejoice and remember the good times and the hard times. We would carry one another's burdens that they might be light, as we covenanted in the waters of baptism. We would bear testimony. But above all, we would drink together from the well of living water that quenches spiritual thirst. Such water is essential to our survival. We cannot live without it.

Along with many others, my husband and I were stunned, sobered, and very sorrowful when we read headlines in the *Deseret News* on Saturday, June 8, 1996: "Boys Rushed for Water in Effort to Save Scout," "Bountiful Scout Succumbs to Heat Exhaustion After Water Runs Out." The article explained that David Philips and his Scout troop did not count on the three days of record-breaking temperatures in the high Arizona desert.

Searching for water in the 112-degree heat, David passed out just 100 yards from the Colorado River and later died. As I read of this tragic occurrence, the loss of a young man's physical life, I pondered the anguish and heartbreak of his sorrowing parents. Yet into my mind came the realization and assurance that this young man lives in another sphere. He continues in his progression. He is all right.

But what of those who die spiritually? Do we know anyone, perhaps even someone who is just a hundred yards from living water, who might be dying of spiritual thirst? Could we ever be in that situation ourselves, suffering from spiritual exhaustion for the lack of living water? Have we not all encountered challenging paths along our journey, times when we feel we are hiking, exhausted, in soaring temperatures?

The news article about the boy's collapse went on to print a list of survival tips for desert hikers. I am impressed that these tips are equally important for those wanting to survive the spiritual deserts we encounter as a part of this mortal journey. Let's consider these life-saving tips from the perspective of living water.

1. *Take more than enough water. Drink at least a gallon a day, more during hot weather.*

How much is a gallon of spiritual water? Can we get it by just taking a sip from the cup? Or do we need to drink deeply from the scriptures and other sources of living water, especially when things get hot?

2. *Pack all your water in. Don't depend on natural sources along the trail. You may be surprised.*

This tip made me think of the need to be spiritually self-reliant, to pack our own living water with us. President Heber C.

Kimball said: "The time is coming when no man or woman will be able to endure on borrowed light. Each will have to be guided by the light within himself. If you do not have it, you will not stand" (as quoted by Harold B. Lee, in Conference Report, October 1955, p. 56). Elder Bruce R. McConkie warned, "Great trials lie ahead. All the sorrows and perils of the past are but a foretaste of what is yet to come, and we must prepare ourselves temporally and spiritually" (address at Regional Representatives seminar, 1979).

3. *Always hike with an experienced guide, one who is familiar with the area.*

As members of The Church of Jesus Christ of Latter-day Saints, we have an infallible guide. We have been given the gift of the Holy Ghost to direct us in all things. We will hear this direction in our mind and in our heart (see D&C 8:2).

As I read the survival tips for desert hikers, the message for me seemed to be: Pray and read your survival manual—your scriptures—a minimum amount every day and more when the temperatures are hot and temptations are strong. This living water will quench spiritual thirst and may save your eternal life.

On a large stone panel at the entrance to the Alberta Temple, near where I was born and raised, there is a carving depicting the woman of Samaria talking with the Savior at the well. I remember standing and pondering that scene even before I had a temple recommend and could go inside the building. Who was this woman, I wondered, that the Savior would meet at the well? What was the message of her story, then and now? We don't even know her name, but that may help us put ourselves in her place and better understand our relationship with the Lord and his unconditional love for each one of us, with all our weaknesses and imperfections, our wrong choices and mistakes.

When we ask questions, we prepare the mind to receive answers. May I suggest a few questions to ponder:

What was the setting for Christ's important message? Did the fact that it took place in Samaria have any special meaning?

What was the conversation between the woman and the Savior? Was it just a social visit?

Who was this woman with whom Jesus chose to share his message of living water, to whom he declared his identity as the Messiah? What difference does it make to know that she was not the Relief Society president or even the wife of the stake president but, in fact, a woman who had made many wrong choices? She wouldn't even have been allowed in the temple at that time in her life, and yet she was the one whom Jesus went out of his way to teach. Why?

What was the difference between the water the Savior offered her and the water she offered him? What does it mean to "never thirst"? Where do we get that kind of water? How much does it cost? Where is the well? Must we go to Samaria, or is it in fact right here?

Will we accept the offer of living water, or by our own choice will we suffer a dry and parched thirst?

Can we collect enough water in pots that our children, our families, will not thirst? Will we teach them of the water so that when we are not there they will be familiar enough with the source to drink freely on their own?

Are there people just a hundred yards from the water that we might rescue if we would?

What was it that the Savior wanted to teach the woman at the well and all of us? Did she learn? Will we?

Now let us turn to John, chapter 4, and learn what we can from the events that took place at the well in Samaria. Jesus and his disciples traveled through Samaria on their way to Galilee. This was not a popular route because of the longtime animosity between the Jews and the Samaritans, who did not often speak to each other. The account states, "And he must needs go through Samaria" (John 4:4). He came to the ancient well of Jacob, which had been known for centuries as an unfailing source of water (think of the symbolism). There, we read, he was "wearied with his journey" and "sat thus on the well" (v. 6). We see the reality of Jesus' mortality as we read of his thirst and weariness. He understands our most basic needs even though he is the Son of God.

Next, "there cometh a woman of Samaria to draw water." It was quite natural that a weary traveler without means to draw water would ask, as Jesus did, "Give me to drink" (v. 7). But her genuine surprise expressed itself in her question, "How is it that thou, being a Jew, askest drink of me, which am a woman of Samaria?" (v. 9). To her question Jesus responded, "If thou knewest the gift of God, and who it is that saith to thee, Give me to drink; thou wouldest have asked of him, and he would have given thee living water" (v. 10).

This response caused her to question, since he had no container with which to draw water. She, of course, was thinking only of the water with which she was familiar, that within the well. But the Savior wanted to raise her to a higher level of understanding. "Whosoever drinketh of this water shall thirst again," he told her. "But whosoever drinketh of the water that I shall give him shall never thirst; but the water that I shall give him shall be in him a well of water springing up into everlasting life" (vv. 13–14). What a message! What a promise! What a precious gift! The Savior wants us to develop within ourselves a living strength that will quench forever our thirst for peace and happiness and eternal life.

However, thinking only of physical needs, the woman of Samaria missed the message. She heard but did not fully understand, and her response was, "Sir, give me this water, that I thirst not, neither come hither to draw" (v. 15). How often do we focus our attention, our petitions on what we think we want, when what he wants for us is so much, much more?

Jesus, knowing that the woman was not understanding him, told her, "Go, call thy husband, and come hither" (v. 16). She responded that she had no husband, and he told her she had had five husbands. Did the Master Teacher reveal this to embarrass her or catch her in sin? No. It was to let her know two things: first, that he was a prophet, and second, that he knew of her weaknesses and still desired to help her find peace and happiness. When the woman bore her testimony of the coming Messiah, he told her, "I that speak unto thee am he" (v. 26).

Finally, this woman of Samaria was no longer concerned for her watering pots. She had been raised to that higher level of understanding. We read that she left her watering pots—she turned away from the physical things that had consumed her attention—to go into town and spread the glad tidings. "Come, see a man, which told me all things that ever I did: is not this the Christ?" she said (v. 29). And how effective was this woman in sharing her marvelous encounter with the Savior and Messiah? Did she worry over whether the people of the town would believe a woman of questionable reputation? Apparently that possibility did not cause her to hesitate in her desire to share the message. She had been touched by the Spirit. Her life was changed. This woman who today would surely be considered "less active" was evidently instrumental in bringing many "unto him" (v. 30). She had partaken of the living water at the well of Jacob.

And where are these wells of living water to be found today? Elder Bruce R. McConkie taught, "Where there are prophets of God, there will be found rivers of living water." Do we fill our buckets from the well of living water at general conference? Do we read the messages of living water in the *Ensign*? Do we attend sacrament meeting weekly and partake of the sacred emblems, living water that quenches spiritual thirst? In our family home evenings and private study, do we drink deeply? Or do we take just a sip from the cup and travel on, sometimes thirsty and weary, despondent and discouraged, perhaps languishing only a hundred yards from the source?

I pray that we might drink from the fountain of living waters and be willing to share these saving truths with others. Let us fill our pitchers, our canteens, our vessels and take the water to those who are suffering, those who would drink but know not where to find the water.

One semester I was teaching an institute class of about a hundred students. As far as I could tell in a group that size, it seemed that everyone was doing reasonably well. I did not observe anyone whose spiritual life seemed to be threatened. But we are not always able to discern the needs of others, as I learned from an anonymous letter I received from a class member. "I have enjoyed your Book of Mormon class immensely," the unknown person wrote. "I feel the Spirit strongly whenever I come into the room. However, there is hardly a moment in my waking life that I am not praying that I could be banished, that I could cease to exist both body and soul. I am not guilty of any great sin that should cause me such profound depression, so I am confused as to why I am so anxious to end my life. I do not want to impose on your limited time, but if you could just think of some suggestion that might help me I would really appreciate it. With love and gratitude, One of your students."

Here was a person who was thirsting. I didn't know who it was; I looked over the class and couldn't tell. How could I draw a bucket of living water to help bring peace to a troubled traveler in the heat of the day? The thought came to me that I might help my struggling friend drink from this living water by reading the words of the Savior: words of encouragement, of promise, of compassion, of mercy and comfort. Praying for guidance as to what might best touch the person's heart, I read into a cassette recorder some of my favorite scriptures, the ones I have marked to read when the heat rises, and others that came to my mind. I ended the tape with my personal testimony and mailed it to the post office box number that had been on the return address of my student's letter.

A week later I received another letter from my anonymous institute student. "Even though I am reluctant to intrude on your limited time," it said, "I feel compelled to thank you for your recorded 'message of hope.' I have kept it in my car and played it several times a day since I received it. Your calm voice charged with testimony and conviction was the strong branch overhanging the river that I clung to to keep from being swept away by the torrential floods of the adversary that washed over me without cessation. Thank you so much for your tape. I will continue to listen to it. I will continue to pray and fulfill all my Church responsibilities. I will make every effort to follow the Master no matter how long the road, how steep the way, or how hot the sun. I will cling to the iron rod."

In the waters of baptism we covenanted to bear one another's burdens and to stand as witnesses of God at all times, in all things, and in all places (see Mosiah 18:8–9). Sometimes we are allowed this sacred privilege without even being aware of it. Even in our imperfections, the Lord will use us as vessels to carry his living water when we are on his errand. When we go forth to do our visiting teaching or our home teaching, for example, it is so much more than a social visit; we are carrying buckets of living water to many who are thirsting. Even the smallest gestures in expression of love can help spread this life-giving substance.

Once, after a speaking engagement in a distant stake, I received a card showing a rather misshapen, awkward-looking turtle with its head barely poking out from the shell. A dear sister had written: "Thank you for visiting our church. I was touched that you cared to ask who I am and spent your valuable time to look at me. I have found it so rare that anyone cares, but a stranger has given me hope. God bless you."

Can a simple look or a smile spread the living water to those who are traveling on steep slopes in the heat of the day? Can you imagine the need of this dear sister who writes, "You spent your valuable time to look at me."

As we travel on the highways of life, let us stop frequently and partake freely from that well of water springing up into everlasting life. Let us share this life-giving moisture with those around us who know not where to find it or who have not the strength to travel the last hundred yards to its source. The supply is never in question unless we ourselves turn off the flow. As we read in the book of Isaiah: "I will pour water upon him that is thirsty, and floods upon the dry ground: I will pour my spirit upon thy seed, and my blessing upon thine offspring" (Isaiah 44:3). Let us drink of that living water from its abundant source and share it with all who come within the sphere of our influence.

INDEX